THE QUIET REBEL

The Quiet Rebel

WILLIAM DEAN HOWELLS

AS

SOCIAL COMMENTATOR

by

Robert L. Hough

UNIVERSITY OF NEBRASKA PRESS

LINCOLN : 1959

The publication of this book was made possible
by a Ford Foundation grant.

Copyright 1959 by the University of Nebraska Press

Library of Congress Catalog Card Number 59-13677

Manufactured in the United States of America

For June

ACKNOWLEDGMENT

The minds and energies of many people have been involved in the writing of this book, and to all of them I wish to acknowledge my deepest gratitude. My debt is especially heavy to William Gibson and George Arms without whose *Bibliography of William Dean Howells* no study of Howells' magazine and newspaper writing would be possible; to Professor Wallace Stegner for his interest, knowledge, and personal counsel which were always available during the writing of the original thesis; to Professors Walter Wright and B. R. McElderry, Jr., for their careful reading and criticism of the book in manuscript; to Professor Robert Knoll for his interest and encouragement; and lastly to my wife June whose work and devotion made this book a reality.

I am also indebted to the Research Council of the University of Nebraska which has provided financial assistance for the final typing of the manuscript and to the Ford Foundation whose grant made publication of the book possible. I am grateful to both these agencies not only for their financial aid but for their continuing interest in the liberal arts.

CONTENTS

THE ZEST FOR CHANGE

ONE FALL AFTERNOON in 1860 a young Midwestern poet was preparing to leave the Concord home of Nathaniel Hawthorne. Upon learning that the young man was next to visit Ralph Waldo Emerson, the white-haired novelist produced one of his cards and wrote on the back, "I find this young man worthy." The trim, small visitor took the card and departed, thrilled by his note of introduction to Emerson, and even more by Hawthorne's kindness and regard.[1]

Hawthorne's judgment about the young man proved to be prophetic for the generations following the Civil War. They too found William Dean Howells worthy, not as a poet to be sure, but as a novelist and an interpreter of the American scene. For thirty years they bought his novels, essays, and reviews when they appeared in the *Atlantic Monthly, Century, Harper's, Cosmopolitan,* the *North American Review,* or in book form. By 1890 Howells was generally recognized as the dean of American letters, a title he was to hold for more than a quarter of a century. In the eyes of his contemporaries, Howells, the leader and promoter of an American school of literary realism, held an importance unsurpassed in the years after the Civil War.

Yet by 1900 Howells' popularity had waned. Industrial Amer-

ica changed rapidly in the years between 1880 and 1900, and
Howells found himself more and more outside its spirit. His
criticism was thought too prudish, too superficial. His fiction
was too timid, too commonplace. In 1911 Harper's discontinued
a Library Edition of his novels partly because the first six vol-
umes had failed to appeal to a generation whose readers had
come to know the more dramatic realism of Norris, Crane, and
Dreiser. Howells himself was acutely aware that his popularity
had declined. In 1916, four years before his death, he wrote to
a friend that *Harper's* no longer wanted his kind of fiction.[2] A
few years earlier he had written to his old companion Henry
James, "I am comparatively a dead cult with my statues cut
down and grass growing over them in the pale moonlight." [3]

Since Howells' death popular opinion has generally supported
this later view. Despite the modern enthusiasm for such nineteenth-century figures as Mark Twain, Henry James, and Her-
man Melville, there have been only a few signs of a serious revival
of Howells' works. It is true that his worth as a social historian
has been recognized, and his position as the principal leader
in the American realistic school has been firmly established by
such scholars as Everett Carter and Gordon Haight.[4] But as a
novelist, Howells has been slighted, despite the fact that peri-
odically some contemporary critic has tried to arouse interest
in him. In 1937 Newton Arvin called him a "decisive figure"
and one that "it was no longer possible to neglect." [5] In 1942
Walter Taylor dealt at length with his artistry and significance.
In 1948 Henry Steele Commager edited a book of selected writings which received praise from book reviewers but disregard
from buyers. And in 1958 Edwin Cady finished the second part
of a perceptive and definitive biography of Howells' life. These
activities, however, have only now begun to stimulate an exam-
ination of Howells' position in American fiction. Generally, except
in period courses in American literature, Howells' writing has received only minor attention from either the reading public or
any large segment of scholars.*

---

* It is too early yet to assess the effect of recent studies done on Howells
by George Bennett, Olov Fryckstedt, and Clara and Rudolf Kirk. It is prob-
able, however, that these books will considerably broaden the current interest in Howells' writing.

Yet there is an important reason that Howells should not be allowed to sink into oblivion. If Howells the social historian remains, so should Howells the social and economic critic. For if the industrialization of the country which followed the Civil War laid the foundations for modern America, as it assuredly did, then Howells, as one of the leading critics of that industrialization, certainly deserves study. Yet this phase of Howells' writing has been curiously neglected. Most critics have passed it by or dismissed Howells as inconsequential.[6] The fact is, however, that Howells was not only one of the best-known novelists in America dealing with social problems during the 1880's and '90's, but also a leading magazine writer who treated such problems prominently in widely circulated journals. This latter point is absolutely vital in any understanding of Howells' social thought because Howells, as the writer of the "Editor's Easy Chair" in *Harper's Monthly,* from 1900 to 1920 continued to press for social reform long after his novels had ceased to speak of it. This fact may be one reason why Howells' ideas are overlooked by critics who read his fiction and conclude that the zest for change dies with *A Traveler from Altruria* in 1894; yet Howells remained engrossed in social problems throughout his life, and some of his bitterest criticism was reserved for the twentieth century. In 1908 he commented on the national government and society in general:

> We are all doing a great deal more for the State than it does for us, and we ought to try, as a matter of duty to one another, to make the State do its part; we ought to educate the State in its duties to the citizens. . . . In its selfishness and meanness it is largely the legislated and organized ideal of the lowest and stupidest of its citizens, whose daily life is nearest the level of barbarism.[7]

It is, of course, impossible to gauge precisely the impact of Howells' thinking on the public of his time. But as an important American novelist he made his ideas known to millions of Americans. As an active contributor to the most reputable magazines in the country and as editor of the *Atlantic* and columnist for *Harper's,* he was in a position of greater prestige and authority than any other reformer of his time and undoubtedly reached circles denied to such critics as Ward, Gronlund, Donnelly, and George. He was a vital part of the great stream of reform that flowed under the surface of American life to emerge with dramatic swiftness in the social changes of the 1930's. Many of his ideas were not original, but his program of reform demonstrates both awareness and insight and represents a real achievement. Literature, he said, should have as its final intention a goal no less than the betterment of the race,[8] and Howells devoted both thought and effort toward the attainment of this end.

2

THE GOLDEN AGE

To UNDERSTAND William Dean Howells' mature social thought, one must begin with his family background and environment in the rural, semi-pioneer villages of Ohio. It is no accident that when Howells came to describe his Utopian state it bore a striking resemblance to the close interdependent life that he had known in the small towns of Hamilton and Jefferson, Ohio, where he had been raised in the 1840's and '50's. Born into a pre-Civil War society, Howells received a picture of life that he never forgot. Later, in the 1880's and '90's, when Bellamy, Macnie, and other American millenniumists were depicting the perfect state of the future as one of science and technology, Howells was depicting it as one of rural calm and cooperation. These men went to the future for their Utopias; Howells went to the past.

Joseph Howells, the novelist's grandfather and the founder of the Howells family in America, was both a drifter and a dreamer. A prosperous woolen merchant, he came to this country from Wales in 1808, determined to make his fortune in a new and growing land, only to find that, despite his best efforts, his means dwindled away. He traveled over much of the eastern United States, looking for the right opportunity—an opportunity which always seemed to elude him. Gradually he sank into the middle class and eventually became the owner of a rural drug, book, and general store in small-town Ohio.

Despite his lack of financial success, Joseph gave his children a firm set of religious ideals. A religious "maverick" (for much of his life he was part Quaker and part Methodist), Joseph believed passionately in the principle of nonviolence and declared himself a pacifist. He hated slavery and in 1815 joined one of the first abolitionist societies in Ohio. He believed in the brotherhood of all men and in cooperation between men. These ideals influenced his oldest son, William Cooper Howells, far more than Joseph's complex system of theological beliefs. William Cooper was stirred by the concept of human brotherhood and by the ideas of individual freedom and personal responsibility, and these were the ideas that William Cooper passed on to his novelist-son, who was to use them as the foundation for his political and social philosophy.

Like his father, William Cooper was also a rover. During the first four years after his marriage to pretty Mary Dean in 1831, William Cooper and his bride lived in seven different towns in Ohio and West Virginia. He was by turns a house painter, a farmer, a general handy man, and a printer during these early years, and even after the family began to arrive, William Cooper continued to travel and change jobs. By the time Howells, born in 1837, was nineteen, the boy had lived in six different towns and seen his father in six different jobs, though the work came increasingly to be connected with printing and publishing.

The idealism that William Cooper learned from his father took similar forms too. Though a tolerant man and one who taught his children tolerance (a trait essential to religious outsiders and to abolitionists in antebellum southern Ohio), William Cooper believed there could be no personal compromise with evil. Other men's opinions, sincerely held, he respected and taught his children to respect, but for himself there could be only one right path in religion, in politics, in personal conduct. This moral absolutism led him into abolition and Swedenborgianism and affected many of his practical decisions. One of the most significant of these occurred in 1848 when William Cooper decided to retire from the editorship of the Hamilton *Intelligencer,* a Whig paper that he had published for eight years, because he could not conscientiously support the Whig presidential candidate, Zachary Taylor. As a young man Taylor had owned slaves, and though his position on the admission of new slave states was not clear, he was suspected of being pro-Southern. Moreover, he was a military man who had gained prominence in the Mexican War, a conflict that the elder Howells thought infamous. In November 1848, with no ready capital and no job in sight, but with a wife and seven children, William Cooper Howells sold out his interest in the *Intelligencer* in an act of protest against his party. Later, when Taylor proved not to be pro-slavery, William Cooper made his peace with the Whig Party, but in the meantime he had lost one of the best positions that he had ever held. It was fully seven years before the Howellses recovered from this decision; yet, as his son later recorded, his father had no "thought of compromising his convictions and his interests" and he displayed on several occasions "that unconscious courage that his life was full of." [1]

In the seven years that followed the *Intelligencer* episode, the elder Howells and his family were often on the brink of poverty, and once, almost in desperation, William Cooper turned to a long-held dream for subsistence. He and his brothers attempted to establish a communitarian society on the banks of the Little Miami River near what is now Xenia, Ohio. The brothers bought an old grist mill, and William Cooper took charge of converting it into a paper mill which was supposed to attract men interested in a cooperative venture. William Cooper had long been impressed by the communitarian ideas of Robert Owen, the English philanthropist, and François Fourier, the French socialist whose concepts of community phalanges and cooperative housing had great influence on the later days at Brook Farm. The elder Howells apparently hoped to use Owen's experiment at New Harmony as a guide, but after eighteen months the plan had to be abandoned for financial reasons. The Howellses' money dwindled away and William Cooper was unable to interest enough "right people" in the project. Despite its failure, however, the plan always held a fascination for the younger Howells. The cooperative principle and a life close to nature appealed to him both as a boy and as a man, and each was to have its place in his later Altruria.

During these years of struggle, Howells was very close to his parents. His mother provided the love and understanding that the small, timid boy needed, and it was to her that Howells turned after his terrible bouts with homesickness. She was responsible for Howells' practicality, which co-existed with his idealism and made him frugal and financially shrewd. It was his father, however, who influenced Howells the most and provided the intellectual stimulus for his inquiring mind. It was he who discussed moral, religious, and philosophical matters with the growing boy and directed Howells' literary interests. Delighted that his son shared his own pleasure in reading, the elder Howells always had a barrel of books around the house, some of which he bought particularly for his son. Howells soon came to enjoy many of William Cooper's literary passions, especially the romantic poetry of Cowper and Burns. Shakespeare, Goldsmith, Cervantes, Irving, Pope, Moore, Byron—the works of all these writers Howells first met at his father's house and talked over with his father in their frequent walks through the rural countryside, another delight of the elder Howells that the boy grew to love. His rambles under the chestnuts and oaks and along the paths and streams of rural Ohio, talking with his father about authors and literature and life—these experiences formed some of Howells' fondest memories of his youth and provided the starting point for his literary ambitions.

II

Howells himself was born in 1837 in the small Ohio river town of Martins Ferry, then known as Martinsville. The second child and the second son in a family of eight children, Howells was a small, frail, blue-eyed towhead. When he was three, he moved with his family to Hamilton, Ohio (population 1,140 in 1840), where his father took up his duties as editor of the Hamilton *Intelligencer*. There he spent the next nine years and the happiest part of his boyhood. Hamilton was much like Mark Twain's

Hannibal, and Howells chronicled the barefoot, carefree part of his youth in *A Boy's Town,* written forty years later.

The boy's education in Hamilton, indeed throughout his school years, was gained primarily at what Lincoln later called "the poor boy's college"—the print shop. Here Howells, from the time he was six, was to read the speeches, the poetry, the news, the stories, the jokes, the ads that went through his father's small-town newspaper office. Like Mark Twain, Walt Whitman, and other writers of his generation, Howells discovered that such reading was in itself a liberal education, and one which gave him a better foundation than he could have received from the rural Ohio schools in the 1840's. Altogether Howells had only about two years of formal schooling, but this fact did not handicap him. In 1851, after spending a few days in a district school near Xenia, Howells returned home, convinced that there was little to be learned at such a school by a member of a reading family such as his.

After William Cooper's resignation from the *Intelligencer* in 1848 and the family's departure from Hamilton, hard times befell the Howellses. All the children worked that could, and the younger ones who could not work took over household duties from the older ones. After a move to Dayton, where the elder Howells acquired an interest in the Dayton *Transcript,* the family burden was intensified. The *Transcript* was a floundering paper, and William Cooper threw all his resources, including his family, into saving it. But fifteen months later, the paper went under, and finally in October 1850, Howells took his family to a one-room log cabin and the social experiment on the banks of the Little Miami.

Again, as we have seen, the Howellses failed. The experiment at the Eureka Mills (an ironic name) was eventually abandoned; but despite this the eighteen months at Xenia were happy ones for Will. He had time to read and to write, activities that had been impossible in Dayton, and he began his studies of language. He grew much closer to his father, who had more leisure and chose to spend it with his family. The long walks, begun in Hamilton, were continued, and William Cooper and his son had a chance to renew their romantic passion for nature.

Eureka Mills marked the low point in the Howellses' fortunes;

from 1851 on, things grew better for the family. From Xenia, William Cooper went to Columbus as a legislative reporter for the liberal *Ohio State Journal* and then to Ashtabula as the new Whig editor of the Ashtabula *Sentinel*. The following year, 1853, the *Sentinel* was moved downstate to the county seat at Jefferson, and the new editor and his family finally found themselves a permanent home. The paper prospered in the congenial atmosphere of the Western Reserve, populated largely by New Englanders who had come down to Ohio through the Great Lakes and whose views on religion and politics often matched those of William Cooper Howells. Young Will had a chance to practice both his journalistic and creative writing as he eventually assumed direction of the literary section of the paper and then took over the editorial page when his father covered the legislative sessions.

During these years, William Cooper's intense interest in politics was communicated to his son. The Republican Party, made up largely of Free Soilers and liberal Whigs and Democrats, was organized in Ohio in the 1850's and assumed power by electing Salmon P. Chase governor in 1855. The *Sentinel* stood firmly behind Chase, and both father and son wrote editorials for his campaign. Howells' interest in politics is further illustrated by two serialized stories that he wrote for the paper in 1854, "A Tale of Love and Politics, Adventures of a Printer Boy" and "The Independent Candidate," the second of which reveals a thorough understanding of practical politics.

In 1857, when Howells was twenty years old, he accompanied his father to Columbus as co-author of a "Letter from Columbus" column for the Cincinnati *Daily Gazette*. William Cooper, now the clerk for the legislature, planned that he and Will would write the column jointly, but soon saw that his son could handle the job alone and happily withdrew, thus launching Howells on a career as a political writer. The zestful and perceptive columns were immediately successful, and the young man slowly began to build a name for himself.

The next three years were important ones for Howells because they furnished him with two invaluable attributes: social polish and influential friends. The social circle in pre-war Columbus bustled with activity, particularly during a legislative session,

and for an obviously talented, marriageable young man the in-
vitations to teas, at-homes, dinners, and parties were almost
without end. Howells met virtually every important public figure
in Ohio, and being young and likeable, he made many close
friends. He knew Governor Chase well enough to borrow books
from his personal library; he was on familiar terms with Benja-
min Wade, a U.S. Senator from Ohio, and with Joshua Giddings,
the powerful antislavery congressman from Ashtabula County.
He knew Henry D. Cooke (Jay Cooke's brother), Judge Swan,
Samuel Smith, and Moncure Conway, all respected men in pre-
war Ohio.

So highly was Howells thought of in his circle that in 1860
western Republicans chose him as the man to write a campaign
history of their candidate for president, Abraham Lincoln, a man
whose background was similar to Howells'.[2] Howells, pleased
at the honor, accepted, but felt he had nothing of the interviewer in him, and so sent a friend to see Lincoln in Springfield,
thus missing, as he put it, "the opportunity of my life." Despite
never meeting his subject, Howells wrote a more than acceptable
biography which sold well and pleased Republican leaders.

This book was the climax of Howells' stay in Columbus. Because of its success and the influence of his friends, he received
an appointment as American consul at Venice from the Lincoln Administration in 1861. In Italy Howells watched for Confederate ships that never came, and completed the polishing
process begun in Columbus. He read, wrote, traveled, went to
theaters and art galleries, met wandering Americans and European cosmopolites. In 1862 he married Elinor Mead, a girl
from a prominent Vermont family, whom he had met in Columbus and who gave him insight into New England and its
traditions and authors.

In 1865, with this augmented background and a publishable
manuscript (Venetian Life), Howells returned to New York and
a post-Civil War America, determined to make his way in the
literary world. But the United States that Howells came back
to was not the same country that he had left. Subtle changes
had occurred during the four years of the Civil War, and these
changes were to have tremendous consequences. To understand
Howells' later career, one must look at both the Americas, the

old and the new, the agricultural and the industrial, because
Howells, perhaps more than any other American writer of his
time, was profoundly influenced by his environment. He was a
product of the Golden Age and the Gilded Age, and each, in a
different way, left its imprint on him.

III

William Dean Howells was brought up in a period known today
as America's "Golden Age," a time of great pride in the United
States and in its achievement of making an equalitarian democracy work. Most young men reared in this environment could
not help absorbing a democratic philosophy. To them equality
was not only social and political, but psychological too. It extended into education, into professional life, and, in the West,
into economics. Many American spokesmen took pride in point-
ing out that America had evolved a truly classless society, one
in which every man was the equal of his neighbor.

A certain amount of this pride was justified. The Ohio in
which Howells grew up was equalitarian both in reality and in
philosophical belief. "Nobody was very rich and nobody was
in want," [3] Howells says of Hamilton in the 1840's, and this was
true of much of the Middle West. There were few millionaires
because there were few ways of making a great deal of money.
There was little destitution because there were few ways of being completely down and out. When in need, a man could always borrow food from his neighbor or hire himself out as a farm
hand or laborer.

The Protestant religion was a major force in promoting this
equalitarianism. In its reaction against priest-led authority, Protestantism stressed the equality of man and the ability of everyone to understand the Holy Word and to obtain salvation
without an intercessor. To non-Calvinistic Protestants, certainly in
the majority during the nineteenth century, no man was in theory
any better than his brother before God. Everyone presumably
worked out his own salvation and no one had favored status.
Howells was firmly in this tradition. His father was a staunch
Swedenborgian and "the children were taught that in every
thought and deed they were choosing their portion with the
devils or the angels." [4] Thus when ministers or circuit-riding

preachers such as Edward Eggleston or his ministerial creations, Kike Lumsden and Mort Goodwin,[5] proclaimed the equality of all men before the Divine Ruler, Howells and others felt they were on firm religious grounds.

Satisfaction with such an equalitarian system was general in the small rural areas and farming communities of the Midwest. Pioneer conditions inevitably level rank and station, and most of the Middle West was in a pioneer or near-pioneer state. Here men were equal in reality as in theory. People had to obtain a living from the soil or from those who did, and Howells tells of his father's exchanging newspaper subscriptions for wood, vegetables, and "every sort of farm produce." [6] Almost everyone had to worry about the weather, about stumps, about cattle, about corn, and about water, whether he was a farmer or a shoemaker. In the isolated and tightly knit communities each man had some obligation to his neighbor, whether it was to help with the harvest or provide a weekly newspaper, and all men were expected to live up to their obligations. There was a "general equality and general dependence of all upon neighborly kindness and good offices of others," William Cooper Howells wrote in 1895.[7]

This does not mean, of course, that there was no independence in rural America. In fact, almost the opposite was true. Ownership naturally encouraged independence, and every man who owned a farm or a country store regarded himself as a free individual. Philosophical convictions strengthened this belief. Protestantism, *laissez faire* economics, and political democracy all stressed man's freedom, and most Americans, farm or city folk, firmly upheld these principles. Henry Steele Commager, writing of rural, pre-Civil War Americans, remarks, "They believed passionately in themselves and their destiny. . . . Born of geography, nourished by history, confirmed by philosophy, self-reliance was elevated to a philosophical creed, and in time individualism became synonymous with Americanism." [8]

The dichotomy that was later to plague industrial America— that of cooperation versus individualism—was noted as early as 1831 by Alexis de Tocqueville. De Tocqueville saw, and Howells was to see later, that Americans had roots imbedded on both sides of the fence. Much of their cooperation Americans put down to "neighborliness." That is, the arrival of a new family

meant that all the townsmen joined in a hard-working but fes-
tive house-raising. When new school buildings or other civic
improvements were necessary, the men were again called upon.
Howells relates how neighbors pitched in and helped build his
father's home at Xenia and how the entire male population of
Hamilton turned out to repair a leak in the town reservoir.[9]
People joined together and formed churches, and then new
churches. The men had their political parties and the women
their quilting societies and church groups. Weddings, school pic-
nics, corn shuckings, and spelling bees were community affairs.
Edward Eggleston in *The Hoosier Schoolmaster* gives a delightful picture of the social aspects of a country spelling bee in
pre-Civil War Indiana, and in *The Circuit Rider* shows the competition and frolicking of a corn shucking.[10] To join was to be a
member of the group, and most rural Americans, individualists
though they were, saw that their lives were enhanced by cooperation with others. Few people would have denied John
Donne's "No man is an island."

Another characteristic of the Midwesterner of the 1850's was
his optimism. Life was getting better, he thought. He had seen
progress right before his eyes in the clearing of the primitive
forests, the coming of the log cabins, the frame houses, the little
villages, and eventually the larger towns. He had seen his own
life made easier through the strides of science and technology.
He had seen great advances in the popularization of knowledge
as books, lyceums, libraries, evening schools, debating societies,
and manuals of self-culture spread rapidly throughout the country. In Columbus, Howells heard Bayard Taylor and Ralph
Waldo Emerson speak in the 1850's in a public lecture series.[11]
Most major cities in the North and Midwest had similar pro-
grams. As far west as Indianapolis there was a good city series
as early as 1855, and Edward Everett, Theodore Parker, and
Ole Bull all visited the Indiana capital. In Cincinnati, Ormsby
Mitchel's talks on astronomy proved so popular that his listeners
banded together in 1846 and bought him a telescope second
to none in the United States.[12] Education brought progress, most
people believed, and with the spread of knowledge went a spread
of optimism. As Howells notes in *Stories of Ohio* (1897), education and the canals were the two roads out of the wilderness

for the early settlers, and they were eager to avail themselves of both.[13]

Along with education, or perhaps because of it, went a great deal of cultural aspiration. The rural handicraft system allowed both business and professional men to enter actively into the political and cultural aspects of the community, and Midwestern society, and American society on the whole, was sincerely concerned with cultural aspiration. In the elder Howells' printing office, there was talk of Tom Paine, Shakespeare, Dickens, the Bible, politics, Swedenborgianism, and morality.[14] Howells relates that all the neighboring farmers came over one summer evening and sat in the gathering twilight to hear him talk of Holmes, Longfellow, and Whittier after he had returned from his first trip to the East.[15] In rural Indiana and Illinois people would travel a hundred miles to attend court and follow the logic and rhetoric of the lawyers. Abraham Lincoln walked miles to borrow a book and then sat up most of the night to read it by firelight. Americans, for the most part, were an inquisitive group, bent on self-improvement and eager to justify their faith in democracy. They believed that man had certain "unalienable Rights" and that with these rights man could do great things. Given the chance, he could prove his goodness.

The philosophic theory that lay behind this faith was inherited from the eighteenth-century Enlightenment and from Newtonian physics. These two doctrines combined to teach that the universe operated by natural laws of cause and effect, that it was figuratively a great machine, which men through study and observation could understand without supernatural guidance. The laws were the natural order of the world, and the closer man could come to them in his economic, social, and political institutions, the more perfect his culture would be. Thomas Huxley summed up this philosophy in 1890 in "Science and Culture." "It is . . . certain," he wrote, "that nature is the expression of a definite order with which nothing interferes, and that the chief business of mankind is to learn that order and govern themselves accordingly." [16]

Since man could learn these laws and test and adjust his institutions by them, it seemed clear that society was ultimately perfectible. If the universe was a great machine, why couldn't society, through science and reason, be made to conform to it? Why couldn't man create an environment in accordance with natural law?

But what was the natural environment for man? What milieu would best place him in harmony with the order of the universe? This was a basic question both in Europe and in America. Largely through the influence of the rising middle classes the concept arose that the most natural environment was one which permitted a great deal of personal liberty.

> They [the seventeenth- and eighteenth-century middle classes] needed to be released from the hampering economic doctrines that a religious and feudal society had imposed against taking interest and "undue" profits. They required not an organic, regulatory state, but one invested with mere police powers. An environment allowing for personal freedom, so necessary to commerce and trade, came to be regarded as the natural environment, the one in accord with the great harmonious mathematical laws of the universe itself.[17]

Certainly such a theory matched the humanistic concept of the inherent worth and dignity of man. The individual, by using his reason and inclination toward the good, could enjoy and profit from personal freedom. Gradually the idea grew that man had certain inalienable rights to life, liberty, property, and the pursuit of happiness. In America this idea found great favor with the independent farmers and merchants of the eighteenth century and was permanently expressed by Thomas Jefferson in the Declaration of Independence. Later it became an ideological foundation for the nineteenth century. Man was good and could do great things with his freedom.

It was this heritage of democracy, of optimism, of equality, that molded the young Howells. He lived his first twenty-four years in rural America of the Golden Age, and it left its mark upon him. When he turned to social criticism in the 1880's he looked at society from the cultural viewpoint of his youth. He realized that matters were not going as he and his generation had confidently predicted. What had happened to America in the thirty years since the Civil War? In 1888 Howells wrote to

Henry James, "After fifty years of optimistic content with 'civilization' and its ability to come out all right in the end, I now abhor it, and feel it is coming out all wrong in the end. . . ." [18]

IV

What had happened was the Industrial Revolution. After the Civil War, America's industrial potential had only to be developed. Protected from foreign wars and international competition, established in a nation full of natural resources and committed to an individualistic tradition, the industrialist had a clear field before him. A growing native population and an increased immigration provided both consumers and laborers. Moreover, the country was psychologically ready for industrial expansion. Wearied of war, people were eager to turn to new enterprises, new goals which promised new benefits. Unfortunately other goals lost ground in the rush of industrial expansion; somewhere along the line culture and reading and breadth of interests became less important to many Americans. Tremendous financial gains became possible, and ambition was primarily stimulated toward such gains.

This shift represents a real change in the American scene. It is true that there was undoubtedly a great deal of materialistic aspiration in the earlier America, and there is ample evidence that ever since the days of the Puritans Americans had been interested in getting ahead financially. But until the Industrial Age there were only two ways of amassing a fortune—commerce and ownership of land—and until an adequate transportation system could be developed, both had inherent limitations. Ambition was often forced into other channels. But with the coming of the railroads and the great expansion of manufacturing made possible by new machines, undreamt-of wealth became pocketable:

> The truth is the close of the war with our resources unimpaired gives an elevation, a scope to the ideas of leading capitalists, far higher than anything ever undertaken in this country before. They talk of millions as confidently as formerly of thousands.[19]

So wrote General John Sherman in 1865, and his words had a prophetic ring.

With governmental encouragement and with improved methods of production, American manufacturing shot ahead tremendously after the Civil War. The steel industry, using the new Bessemer process and the open hearth, sprang from an annual production of 2,600 tons in 1867 to 375,000 tons in 1875 to 929,000 in 1879.[20] A giant had come from nowhere. Production was multiplied 360 times, and in the twelve years between 1867 and 1879 the greatest American steel companies were firmly established. Thousands of men found work in the newly opened plants. In addition, steel production aided railroad expansion and the development of iron mines in Michigan and Minnesota. It also encouraged manufacturing and agricultural production because the durability of steel rails soon lowered transportation costs. By furnishing a better and more adaptable product, steel producers stimulated the entire American economic system.

The growth of the steel industry, however, was no more marvelous than that of other enterprises. The petroleum industry, for example, came from even more obscure beginnings than steel. The first well was not sunk in the United States until 1859, when Colonel E. L. Drake decided the black oozy liquid he saw around him in Titusville, Pennsylvania, had value. Then with the discovery of oil as an efficient lubricant and illuminant, production boomed. By 1864, only five years after the first well, 2,100,000 barrels were being taken from the earth yearly, and by 1870 the figure had risen to over five million barrels.[21] New towns sprang up where prairies or farm lands had been. People flocked to the oil fields to work in refineries and to look for oil themselves. Companies formed and re-formed as petroleum became the greatest speculative gamble on the Eastern stock market. By 1870, millions of dollars had been made on what eleven years before had been a bother to farmers and an ingredient in quack medicines. Petroleum had climbed to fourth on the nation's list of export by 1870, and as time passed and more uses of oil and its by-products were discovered, production and exportation continued to rise. By 1880 almost 24,500,000 barrels were coming from wells annually, and the crude oil itself was valued at $22,700,000.[22]

Such industrial change naturally resulted in social change. Henry Adams, looking back over the nineteenth century from the vantage point of the twentieth, remarked that, in all concepts of science and technology, 1854 was nearer to the year one than to the year 1900.[23] The economic and social change in the nineteenth century was almost as prodigious. Adams believed that the society of the 1850's was ruled by men of thought and intellect, the Emersons, the Websters, the Channings. But two decades later he acknowledged that new rulers had appeared, the men of business and energy, the moneymakers, the industrialists.[24] He saw that the Rockefellers, the Hills, and the Vanderbilts were becoming the social idols. To Adams this was not just change but revolution.

3

HOWELLS AND THE ATLANTIC

IN 1865 William Dean Howells returned to the United States after four years in Italy. The years had been rewarding ones; the leisure for reading and travel, the familiarity with European art and artists, and the close study of Italian poetry and drama all had their effect on a man as perceptive as Howells. But it is clear from Howells' two books, *Venetian Life* and *Italian Journeys,* that the years in Italy had little impact on his social views. In these books Howells is far more interested in cultural and literary matters than in social or economic ones. There are many comments on churches, castles, art galleries, and national shrines, but few, if any, on crime, housing, or employment. Nor is it logical to expect anything else from a rurally raised young man with a burning desire to be an American poet.

Howells' education in social problems began when he returned to New York and, after some job-searching, landed a position as reporter and columnist for E. L. Godkin's *Nation.* In writing his "Minor Topics" column for Godkin, Howells touched upon such matters as labor problems, criminal justice, and model tenements,

though never with great insight.[1] Yet had Howells remained
longer in New York (he was there only five months), he might
have seen certain problems earlier and more clearly than he did.
His job brought him into contact with aspects of life that he
had never seen before, and association with Godkin and his circle undoubtedly would have proved stimulating. But Boston
and a better job beckoned, and Howells moved on to the *Atlantic
Monthly* and to new duties before his own writing could show
real social concern. His New York experiences were too few and
too early, both for Howells' awareness and for the worst mani-
festations of industrialism.

In New England Howells led much the same kind of quiet,
peaceful life he had known in the small villages of Ohio. To be
sure, the intellectual stimulation was greater in Cambridge
where the Howellses made their new home, but the social atmosphere was similar to what Howells had known before. Closely
associated with Harvard College, Cambridge society was generally one of civilized equality where men met and talked freely
regardless of station or rank.[2] In such a society Howells felt at
home. He met on Wednesday evenings with Longfellow's Dante
Club where ten or twelve of the best Italian scholars in America
listened and offered suggestions as the poet read his translation
of Dante. He was constantly in the company of Lowell, his clos-
est friend during the Cambridge years. He took long walks and
discussed art with Henry James. He knew John Fiske and Louis
Agassiz and Charles Eliot Norton. He was intimately acquainted
with the intellectual life of Harvard, giving talks and attending
functions there. Although Boston was only seven miles away
and Howells journeyed there during the week, his writings
during the late '60's and early '70's show no urgent awareness
of the problems of the growing city—its industrial expansion, its
increasing population, its corruption. Instead, his pictures of
Boston in *Suburban Sketches* (1871) are full of horsecars, sec-
ond-hand stores, servant types, and walking trips. He does see
and comment on the slums and the factories, but he shows no
understanding of their significance. He talks at some length
about the clustering Irish dwellings, but there is no recognition
of what they portend.[3]

II

In July 1871 Howells, then thirty-four, became editor of the *Atlantic Monthly,* succeeding James T. Fields and inheriting the most influential literary journal in America.[4] Reorganized in 1857, the *Atlantic* had achieved national prominence under its first two editors, James Russell Lowell and Fields, and such New England writers as Holmes, Emerson, Hawthorne, Whittier, and Longfellow took an almost proprietary interest in its success. The *Atlantic,* however, was more than a literary journal; its subtitle, "A Magazine of Literature, Science, Art and Politics," indicates its emphasis on contemporary affairs. After a five-year apprenticeship as assistant editor, Howells knew both the pattern and the contributors of the magazine and was able to assume his new duties without noticeable confusion or change. The first issues under his editorship had their usual quota of well-known writers—Dana, De Forest, Longfellow, Harte, and Higginson were all represented in Howells' first number—and the customary features were evident throughout.[5]

Each issue of the *Atlantic* at this time contained four or five poems, four or five stories (including serials), and six or seven articles of general interest. Howells continued this general pattern throughout the early years of his editorship. One article in each issue generally concerned some broad social question and was written by a well-known author or expert on that topic. For example, in the six months between January and June 1874, these five articles appeared in the magazine: Louis Agassiz's "Evolution and Permanence of Type"; David Wells' "A Modern Financial Utopia" and "The Theory and Practice of Local Taxation in the United States"; James Layard's "Morphine"; and George Cary Eggleston's "A Rebel's Recollections," a personal and sociological picture of the South during the Civil War.[6]

As the years passed it became increasingly evident that by the very fact of editing a journal of "science, art, and politics," Howells was forced to reflect upon contemporary problems. Of course there is no evidence to show that he was not being immersed in current events through other means, but the *Atlantic* was undoubtedly a great stimulus to his thinking. He was constantly soliciting articles for the magazine. "Do you know a good man to write about the tariff and the silver question—a man for each?" he wrote to his friend James Garfield in 1877.[7] He persuaded George Cary Eggleston, a former Confederate soldier, to write of the South, and obtained essays from Charles Francis Adams, Jr., on the railroads and from Brooks Adams on taxation. He himself wrote articles critical of both Grant and Greeley, the presidential candidates in 1872.[8] Throughout the 1870's he accepted articles on civil service reform, taxation, free trade, specie payment, immigration, transportation, and feminism. One could hardly read, much less edit, the *Atlantic* during these years without gaining a liberal education about contemporary America. Moreover, in the late '70's Howells gradually added a greater emphasis on topicality. Beginning in 1877, the year of the great railroad strike, he conducted an informal forum on the causes of depression and accepted articles approving of credit unions, the establishment of marketing corporations, and new laws for the public domain.[9] Now instead of one article a month on contemporary problems there were often two, bearing such titles as "The Abolition of Poverty," "A Workingman's Word on Over-Production," "Equality," "Socialism in Germany," and "Children's Labor: A Problem." [10] With the growing interest of the *Atlantic* in current affairs goes an interest in the more human side of these problems. The article "Children's Labor" is particularly arresting in its description of the evils of child labor and the frank admission that such work is necessary to sustain some families.

The pieces are provocative; they display a greater interest in social problems than the magazine had yet revealed, and they do advocate some changes, but they are not radical. The article "Socialism in Germany" (October 1879), for example, calls attention to the rising interest in socialistic practices throughout the world and to the advantages such practices have brought. But it mainly shows the weaknesses of socialism—the expensiveness, the bureaucracy, the potential tyranny, and limitation of human freedom—weaknesses which would disqualify it for use in a democratic country. The author, Willard Brown, ends with an affirmation of the American system and the belief that for the present we must fall back on the hope that progress will bring to man the desire and pride of giving to the world as much as has been received.[11]

III

Though an editor cannot be held accountable for the opinions expressed in articles that he accepts, there is independent evidence to suggest that Howells' own views were becoming more searching. His review of J. B. Harrison's *Certain Dangerous Tendencies in American Life, and Other Papers,* a book that was serialized in the *Atlantic* in 1878, strongly suggests the similarity between the editorial policy of the magazine and his personal views.[12] This review, written for the June 1880 issue, contains the most significant social statement that Howells made during his editorship of the *Atlantic.*[13] It concerns eight articles that had been written for the *Atlantic* by a Cambridge minister whom Howells had grown to admire. The essays explored American industrialization and the relationship between management and labor, and sought some basis of reconciliation for the growing conflict between the two. The author believed both sides at fault for strikes and violence but placed primary blame on the strikers who were often ignorant and badly led.[14] He cautioned both groups against their extremist elements and stressed the means by which capital and labor could live side by side—the taking of smaller profits, simpler living, a return to religion, and a greater diffusion of knowledge concerning the problems faced by each group.

Howells praised the articles warmly, calling them "clear, penetrating studies of American life."[15] He countered the charge that the articles were pessimistic by remarking that if pessimism could bring such acuteness, "by all means let us have nothing but pessimism hereafter."[16] He lauded the author for advocating "good reading and good preaching," and for his idea that something more than work was necessary to solve industrial problems. Altogether, it is obvious that Howells agreed with much of Harrison's thinking.

But the emphasis in the review is even more enlightening. Howells often used a review to introduce or reinforce his own ideas, and here he stresses the notion that the problems facing America were fundamental rather than temporary. He wrote:

> Events move so rapidly with us, and superficially conditions change so suddenly, that with the present return of prosperity we shall be in danger of regarding the tendencies and characteristics of American life which this writer deplores as merely traits of the long period of adversity which is passing away. But what this essayist strives to do throughout is to persuade his reader that the relief which may come from better times is temporary and delusive; that hard times will return in their course, and then all the dangerous tendencies of two years ago will beset us again.[17]

While it is true that Harrison does imply that industrial problems are more than superficial, this idea is not specifically stated and is not the main concern of the author, who is more interested in setting down definite recommendations for a new rapprochement between capital and labor. The fact that Howells emphasizes the idea indicates independent thinking. He seems to combine Harrison's thought with his own and issues the result as a warning to the American people that all is not perfect in the capitalistic system.

Later, in December of 1880, Howells accepted for publication "Story of a Great Monopoly," Henry D. Lloyd's exposé of the ruthless practices of the huge Standard Oil Company. The *Atlantic* had printed articles which criticized business before but never one so damning as Lloyd's.[18] The impact on the country of Lloyd's disclosures of secret rebates, extortion, bribery, and perjury was considerable. An unprecedented seven printings of the magazine had to be run off before the demand was satisfied, and Lloyd's article was widely reprinted in newspapers, particularly in the West.[19] It is, of course, significant that the forerunner of the muckraking articles should appear in a magazine edited by William Dean Howells. To accept such an essay in 1880 took a great deal of courage, for Americans, proud of their progress and material wealth, often looked upon the big corporations and trusts as major contributors to this advancement.[20] Yet Howells apparently took the risk with no misgivings. In December 1880 he wrote Lloyd, "I accept your paper with pleasure, and will give it first place in the *Atlantic* for March." [21]

Thus it seems clear that some sort of social consciousness can be detected in Howells during the years 1878-80. Both the articles that he accepted as editor for the *Atlantic* and his own review of Harrison's work reveal an increasing knowledge of the complexities of industrial society and a deepening concern for America's future. Howells was beginning to see faults, and though his insight was not immediately followed by action, it did indicate a watchfulness, a social perceptiveness which the author had not revealed before. In short, Howells' work on the *Atlantic,* which had brought him into close contact with contemporary America, had also brought him his first concern about that America and its economic system.

In his novels of the period Howells reveals these same stirrings of awareness. Here, however, the concern is pronounced only after 1880; the early books, *A Chance Acquaintance* (1873), *A Foregone Conclusion* (1875), and *The Lady of the Aroostook* (1878), are almost devoid of any kind of serious social criticism, though all three glance at class division for the purpose of humor and satire. Nor does *The Undiscovered Country* (1880) offer a great deal more. It mentions the growing number of tramps roaming the countryside but only notes them. It is not until one comes to *Dr. Breen's Practice* and *A Modern Instance,* two novels written immediately after Howells left the *Atlantic* in 1881, that he finds more extended comment. In both books there are significant remarks on divorce and the personal and social problems involved in separation.[22] In *Dr. Breen's Practice* a central theme is the whole question of woman's place in the new society, and in *A Modern Instance* Howells discusses the growing influence of advertisers and manufacturers on newspaper policy, the increasing tendency on the part of owners and writers to regard the newspaper simply as a means to make money, and the pandering to public taste by the theaters and churches.[23]

Two of the questions, divorce and a woman's place in society, figure prominently in the novels, and though the questions of newspaper policy and pandering to public taste are never the motivating forces that other problems will become later, they do aid in characterizing Howell's figures. Bartley Hubbard, for example, is a scoundrel in *A Modern Instance* because he is a creature of capitalism who believes that a newspaper is a private enterprise designed for financial gain and that editors should thus guard the interests of their advertisers. These ideas were particularly odious to an old journalist like Howells, who always feared that the "counting-room morality" would engulf journalistic ideals and a paper's responsibility to its readers.[24]

In summary, it seems fair to say that in 1881 the love for the old America was still strong in Howells, but like others, he was beginning to see that the new reality was different from the earlier dreams. Defects had appeared in the system and gave indications of growing larger and more threatening as time passed. Violence, class bitterness, strikes, depressions had arisen in the new era, and Howells was troubled by what he saw. He closed his review of Harrison's book with these words:

> . . . returning prosperity has put us all in good humor and everyone has apparently come to a clearer perception of things. But very possibly he [Harrison] might insist that this was a transitory and illusory appearance; and that the supine acquiescence of those who confide in it was material for a still more discouraging paper than any he had yet written.[25]

A year later in commenting on the Boston police courts, he remarked,

> Nothing struck me more forcibly in the proceedings of the police court than their apparent futility. It was all a mere suppression of symptoms in the vicious classes, not a cure. . . . These bad boys and girls came up and had their thrashing or their rap over the knuckles, *and were practically bidden by the conditions of our civilization to go and sin some more* [italics supplied].[26]

The seeds of doubt were being sown.

IV

In July 1882, freed of "the continual fret of editorial duties" by his resignation from the *Atlantic*, Howells sailed for Europe, where he and his family spent a year visiting friends in Italy and touring England, France, and Germany. As a good travel writer, he was interested in getting his experiences on paper as soon as he returned. Having remarked that an idea was like a pig—a writer had better pen it while he can—he was eager to record the scenery, the people, the impressions of his trip. Thus there is a brief interim after 1882 when Howells' writing is largely free of comment on the American scene. "A Florentine Mosaic," *Tuscan Cities,* and *Indian Summer,* a novel set in Italy, all concern Europe and only incidentally refer to America. Much of the periodical writing also has little to do with American conditions.

In only one article did Howells make any signficant social comment. This was in a review of John Hay's anonymously published novel, *The Breadwinners,* a strike story which had been criticized for its antilabor views. Howells defends Hay by noting that the author "shows no strong antipathy to strikers till they begin to burn and rob and propose to kill." [27] Violence hurts any cause, Howells points out, but he makes clear that neither he nor Hay favors the employer over the worker. He remarks that in itself working does not sanctify anyone, and he warns against making an idol of the working man. But he carefully notes that employers are responsible for strikes too. He writes, "We should have been well content to see the strikes of the telegraphers succeed and not ill-pleased to see those who thought them well paid enough put to live awhile on their wages." Throughout the article Howells holds to this idea—there is blame on both sides. He condemns alike "the idle rich" and "the idle poor" and tries to view the situation objectively. The problem is obviously complex.

In 1884 Howells finished *The Rise of Silas Lapham,* a fine novel which touches but never explores economic matters. Howells is more concerned with the moral rise of Silas and with the antisentimental conclusion of the Irene-Tom-Penelope triangle than he is with Lapham's business dealings. Silas' connection with Rogers and his involvement with the railroad, two episodes which might have led to a thorough discussion of business practices, are never exploited.

Nevertheless the year 1884 was a crucial one for Howells. Though for the moment his writings do not show it, the novelist apparently reached a point where he could no longer put aside certain questions. For Howells, conditions continued to worsen with no possibility of relief in sight. Twelve years later, in a personal interview for *Harper's Weekly,* he was to tell his readers of the significance for him of 1884. The interviewer wrote:

Howells' socialism is an answer to grave questions which have arisen in the author's own mind; it is offered as a partial solution of problems which he found confronting himself, compelling attention, refusing to be curtly dismissed. They made their demands—these questions—when Mr. Howells was writing *Silas Lapham* in the late summer and fall of 1884. His affairs prospering, his work marching as well as his heart could wish, suddenly, and without apparent cause, the status seemed wholly wrong. His expression, in speaking about that time, was, "The bottom dropped out!" [28]

V

Howells' course of action after 1885 differed markedly from that of the previous years. After 1885, not a single year went by until Howells' death in 1920 without his having some significant comment on American economic and social conditions. His six social novels which span the period 1888-93 placed him firmly in the reform movement which began in the late '80's, and this was a movement that Howells was never really to leave.

The major influences on Howells during the period immediately after 1885, and the sources of his socialism, have received considerable attention in recent years, and it is not necessary to repeat the work of such scholars as Everett Carter and L. J. Budd.[29] Writing in 1897, Howells says of his socialism:

It was ten years ago that I first became interested in the creed of Socialism. I was in Buffalo when Laurence Gronlund [an American Socialist] lectured there before the Fortnightly Club. Through this address I was led to read his book, "The Cooperative Commonwealth," [sic] and Kirkup's article in the *Encyclopaedia Britannica.* Afterwards I read the "Fabian Essays" [sic]; I was greatly influenced also by a number of William Morris's tracts. The greatest influence, however, came to me through Tolstoy. Both as an artist and as a moralist I must acknowledge my deep indebtedness to him.[30]

In brief, what happened was this. Howells apparently came to know Tolstoy sometime during the middle months of 1885. He was impressed by *The Cossacks* and turned to *Anna Karenina*. This story of a vain attempt to find a purely personal happiness affected him tremendously, perhaps because his father's Swedenborgianism had taught him that selfishness was the greatest of all sins and always led to unhappiness.* He wrote to his friend, Thomas Perry, who had first urged him to read Tolstoy:

> Anna Karenina is a wonderful book. I seem to live in it. I don't think it is so great as Tourgueniff's, but the subtlety of the observation in it is astounding, simply . . . how good you feel the author's heart to be; and what a comfort, what a rest that is.[31]

Howells became an avid reader of Tolstoy, going through most of his published works. The extent of this interest can be measured in some way by Howells' writing in 1887. In February he reviewed Tolstoy's *Deux Generations* and *The Death of Ivan Ilyitch* for his "Editor's Study" in *Harper's;* [32] in April he wrote

---

* The influence of Swedenborgian thought on Howells' own ideas has interested several scholars in recent years. Edwin Cady has made the most serious and satisfying study of the relationship; his remarks are to be found in his book *The Road to Realism: The Early Years of William Dean Howells,* pp. 16-22. In brief, Howells and his father seemed to have been moved by the ethical rather than the mystical side of the Swedish reformer's views. The importance of love, the doctrine of salvation through works, the freedom of the will, the morality of the universe, the belief that evil originates in man's self-love—these are the ideas that appealed to Howells and influenced his later thinking. For comment on the theme of self-love which runs through several of Howells' novels, see Cady's remarks noted above. The idea that the universe was moral also found a specific place in Howells' later work. This concept, one he also found in Emerson, gave philosophic backing to Howells' theory of realism in that it provided an ethical basis for depicting things exactly as they were. For Howells, the function of the novel was to be true to life, and if moral and ethical meanings could be gained from man's life (and for most of his life Howells believed they could), then the novelist could be most instructive, most meaningful when he pictured life truthfully. (See *Criticism and Fiction,* 233 ff.)

On the other hand, Swedenborg's allegorical interpretation of Genesis in the *Heavenly Arcana,* his reliance on revelation, and his system of "natural correspondences" between man, nature, and God had little discernible effect on the future novelist.

an article on Tolstoy for *Harper's Weekly;* [33] in May he included in the "Editor's Study" a letter from De Forest on Tolstoy; [34] in July he reviewed *Que Faire?,* Tolstoy's ethical and economic study of industrialism; [35] in August he discussed Tolstoy in connection with the economic levels of the American reading public; [36] and in October he inserted into his column the comments of M. J. Savage on Christ and Tolstoy.[37] Small wonder that Charles Eliot Norton should say in 1887 that Howells had a bad case of Russian measles. [38]

Tolstoy's influence on Howells was primarily one of reviving, at a time of stress, some of Howells' earlier beliefs. L. J. Budd, a scholar who has studied both authors, writes:

> Essentially, Howells learned nothing completely new from Tolstoy. From his youth onward, he had felt that the moral code which had been promulgated by Christ and the Gospels of the New Testament was a sufficient guide for conduct. Neverthless, he found in Tolstoy's work a tremendously appealing restatement of his quiet belief and also an impassioned warning that currently civilization had departed from Christian ethics. . . . Whenever Howells spoke at length concerning Tolstoy, he invariably observed that the Russian had, through his writing and his life, demonstrated the truth and practicability of New Testament teachings.[39]

What Tolstoy did was to revitalize and redirect some of the Christian ethics that Howells had learned as a child. These ethics originated in the devout Swedenborgianism of his father and in the religious training that Howells received in a "very religious household." [40] The nightly readings from the Bible or Swedenborg's *Heavenly Arcana* and his father's personal philosophy of tolerance and ethical action imbued the young Howells with a faith in Christian morality. Renunciation of selfishness; belief in the simple working life; and faith in what one held to be right [41] were all taught the Howells children, and these beliefs were specifically emphasized by Tolstoy. The Russian's repudiation of industrial society, based as it was on Christian tenets, held real meaning for Howells, and the doubts about American capitalism that had stirred uneasily in Howells' earlier writings suddenly crystallized after he read Tolstoy's books. Howells wrote:

> Tolstoy gave me heart to hope that the world may yet be made over in the image of Him who died for it. . . . He taught me to see life not as a chase for an impossible personal happiness, but as a field of endeavor towards the happiness of the whole human family. . . . He gave me new criterions, new principles, which, after all were those that are taught us in our earliest childhood, before we can come to the evil wisdom of the world.[42]

Later he said:

> His writings and his life have meant more to me than any other man's . . . . It has been his mission to give men a bad conscience, to alarm them and distress them in the opinions and conventions in which they rested so comfortably.[43]

But Howells, as we have seen, had not rested comfortably in the conventions of industrialism. And now more than other men he had a bad conscience. But what was to be done? Would it help to reject society and earn one's bread by manual labor as Tolstoy had? Edward Everett Hale met Howells in May 1887, and reported that Howells was deep in Tolstoy and "does not know but he ought to be ploughing and reaping." [44] But this idea of withdrawal, if ever taken seriously, was soon dismissed. In *Annie Kilburn* (1888), the Reverend Peck leaves his pastorate for more practical social work among the industrial poor, and in *The World of Chance* (1892) Howells openly criticizes Tolstoy for his retreat from society and remarks that the world can be reformed only from within, not from without.[45]

But how does one attack a problem of social change? As yet Howells had no answer of his own, but under the impetus of his own misgivings and those of Tolstoy, he set out to find what he could.

The first results of his investigation appeared in February 1886, when Howells published *The Minister's Charge*. He had begun this book two years before, but he and Henry Mills Alden, the editor of *Harper's Monthly*, had not agreed on the story, and Howells, after finishing what he called "my opening chapter," put it aside for a time. When he resumed work on the book in 1885, he was deep in his reading of Tolstoy and may have incorporated some ideas suggested to him by Tolstoy. References to the growing inequality of society and the general public disdain of those who work with their hands are reminiscent of Tolstoy; so is the thought that people can know and sympathize with each other only when their circumstances are similar.[46]

But *The Minister's Charge* has an importance beyond these hints of Tolstoyan influence. The book shows that Howells was moving toward socialism, or at least the implications of socialism, before the Haymarket affair and before Laurence Gronlund's talk in Buffalo. Both of these events undoubtedly had an effect on Howells, but they did not determine the direction of his thought. In *The Minister's Charge,* Evans, a choral character for the author, says:

> . . . don't you see that in establishing and regulating a place like that [a community house for the unemployed] the city of Boston has instinctively sanctioned my idea of community cooperation? You may say that it is aiding and abetting the tramp-nuisance by giving vagrants food and shelter, but other philosophers will contend that it is—blindly perhaps—fulfilling the destiny of the future State, which will at once employ and support all its citizens. . . .[47]

This idea is constantly re-echoed in Howells' later novels, particularly in the Altrurian romances, and is one of the most firmly held of his economic beliefs. In *The Minister's Charge* he reveals that though ignorant of formal doctrine he does accept one of socialism's cardinal tenets—that of public employment and maintenance—as early as 1886.

The concept of what Howells called "complicity" is also broached here for the first time. The conviction that all men are affected by social evil whether they are personally involved in it or not is emphasized throughout the book. The streetcar conductor comments that a man cannot even steal without casting aspersions on others and bringing on new regulations.[48] Evans remarks that the buying and selling of votes affect everyone in a democratic nation.[49] And the Reverend Sewell in a climactic sermon preaches that all men are bound together for good or ill:

> No man . . . sinned or suffered to himself alone; his error and his pain darkened and afflicted men who never heard of his name. If a community was corrupt, if an age was immoral, it was not because of the vicious, but the virtuous who fancied themselves indifferent spectators. . . . The Gospel—Christ—God, so far as men had imagined him—was but a lesson, a type, a witness from everlasting to everlasting of the Spiritual unity of man. . . . Happy he in whose ears their [the wretched's] cry for help was a perpetual voice, for that man whatever his creed, knew God and could never forget him. In his responsibility for his weaker brother he was Godlike, for God was but the impersonation of loving responsibility, of infinite and never-ceasing care for us all.[50]

Here Howells ties the concept of social responsibility to a religious framework, rather than to any political ideology. Man should help his brother because he is his brother's keeper and a follower of Christ, not because he is part of a certain kind of governmental system. Howells' social interest here is humanitarian rather than political. The industrializing, urbanizing change in society has caused some dislocations, and it is for the individual to remedy these whenever he can. There is no concerted protest against business practices in *The Minister's Charge*, although Howells does note that the streetcar company is out to get all it can.[51] His interest is rather in the entire society. He feels that improvement can be made within the present system if men become more conscious of their Christian obligations.

In 1886 Howells' feelings crystallized around a tragic event. A bomb was dropped in the midst of a police troop dispersing a labor protest meeting in Chicago's Haymarket Square, a bomb that killed six and wounded over fifty. The anger, the hatred, the frustration over industrial strife that had been building up in the public mind erupted overnight. Vigilante committees roamed the streets of Chicago looking for labor sympathizers, and the next day newspapers throughout the nation demanded immediate action against anarchists and socialists. The entire country seemed to demand retribution. Eight well-known anarchists were eventually seized in Chicago and tried upon the charge that their speeches and literature were accessory to the fact of murder. The prosecution made no attempt to prove the defendants had dropped the bomb but contented itself with establishing the inflammatory nature of their expressed beliefs. All eight were convicted and seven were sentenced to die.

Howells became interested in the case after reading through the trial record sometime in late 1886 or early 1887. Convinced that the accused had not received a fair trial, he wrote in September 1887 to Judge Pryor, the anarchists' counsel, who was appealing the case to the Supreme Court:

> I am glad you have taken the case of the Chicago anarchists, and that you see some hope for them before the Supreme Court, for I have never believed them guilty of murder, or of anything but their opinions, and I do not think they were justly convicted.[52]

Pryor thanked Howells and suggested that a public statement of his views would do their cause a great deal of good. Howells, however, was at first reluctant to take such action. He asked Pryor not to publish a letter from him on the anarchists, and the judge complied, saying, "No man should challenge public obloquy without a commensurate object." [53] Howells then turned to his old friend, John Greenleaf Whittier, in hopes of gaining an appeal for clemency. But the aged poet, Quaker though he was, refused to protest against the death penalty and advised Howells to write the appeal himself. George William Curtis, to whom Howells looked next, also refused.[54]

Finally, on November 4, two months after he had originally written Judge Pryor and two days after the Supreme Court had confirmed the death sentence, Howells acted. He first petitioned the governor of Illinois to commute the death penalty to imprisonment, and then in a courageous move he wrote a public letter to the New York *Tribune* urging that others join in a campaign to save the anarchists' lives:

. . . I conjure all those who believe that it would be either in-
justice or impolicy to put them to death, to join in urging him
[the governor] by petition, by letter, through the press, and
from the pulpit and the platform to use his power, in the only
direction where power can never be misused, for the mitiga-
tion of their punishment.[55]

This and other appeals were partially successful. Two of the
sentences were changed to life imprisonment, but the other five
were allowed to stand. A few days before the execution date, one
of the convicted men killed himself in his cell with a homemade
bomb. Then on November 11, 1887 the other four were led into a
Chicago jail yard and hanged—an act that Howells called "forever damnable before God and abominable to civilized men." [56]
    In his letters that immediately followed the execution, Howells
was obviously upset. In a penetrating letter-editorial to his old
friend Whitelaw Reid, the publisher of the New York *Tribune*
(a letter which Howells apparently never sent), the novelist
told the American people they all had a part in a "monstrous"
deed:

> We have committed an atrocious and irreparable wrong. We
> have been undergoing one of those spasms of paroxysmal right-
> eousness to which our Anglo-Saxon race is peculiarly subject, and
> in which, let us hope, we are not more responsible for our ac-
> tions than the victim of *petit mal*. Otherwise, we could not for-
> give ourselves; and I say we, because this deed has apparently
> been done with the approval of the whole nation. . . . Under
> the forms of law, their trial has not been a trial by justice, but
> a trial by passion, by terror, by prejudice, by hate, by news-
> paper.[57]

Later he wrote his sister that "it's all been an atrocious piece of
frenzy and cruelty, for which we must stand ashamed forever
before history." [58] Earlier in the same letter, he said:

> Elinor and I both no longer care for the world's life and would
> like to be settled down very humbly and simply, where we could
> be socially identified with the principles of progress and sym-
> pathy for the struggling masses.[59]

Finally, in January 1888, two months after the hangings, he posted a long letter to Hamlin Garland which reveals an intensified feeling:

> You'll easily believe that I did not bring myself to the point of openly befriending those men who were civically murdered in Chicago for their opinions without thinking and feeling much, and my horizons have been indefinitely widened by the process. Your land tenure idea is one of the good things which we must hope for and strive for by all the good means at our hands. But I don't know that it's the first step to be taken; and I can't bring myself to look upon confiscation in any direction as a good thing. The new commonwealth must be founded in justice even to the unjust, in generosity to the unjust rather than anything less than justice . . . . I am reading and thinking about questions that carry me beyond myself and my miserable literary idolatries of the past; perhaps you'll find that I've been writing about them. I am still a slave of selfishness, but I am no longer content to be so.[60]

VI

Other influences undoubtedly had much to do with Howells' new feelings. Social agitation was increasing. A steady decline in farm prices, the beginning of a prolonged drought in the West, the increased labor-management friction, the growing number of novels critical of economic practices—all these contributed to the discontent of the late '80's. Ill feeling spread among factory workers, and during 1886, laboring groups went on strike against 10,057 commercial and manufacturing firms.[61] These strikes, connected mainly with the demand for an eight-hour day, opened ugly breaches between employer and worker, and Howells was undoubtedly aware of the new tensions. In 1888 he moved to New York, a center of strike violence, and there witnessed the bitterly fought streetcar strike which he later depicted in *A Hazard of New Fortunes.*

In the light of these facts, it is reasonable to believe that Howells' change of mind was due to a combination of causes rather than to any single event. But one thing is certain—by the end of 1888 the optimistic, the economically conservative Howells had completely disappeared. In looking over the author's correspondence, one is struck by the fact that the letters written during these twelve months are more pessimistic about American institutions than any he had ever written before, indeed that they show a definite break with the status quo. In April, he wrote Mark Twain that labor was at last educating itself, that workers would begin to win strikes soon, and that the public was betrayed by the press.[62] Later in the same month he told Thomas Perry that he cared little for either political party but would vote for a labor group if one would come forth with any practical ideas.[63] In August he wrote Edward Everett Hale that "our competitive civilization is a state of warfare and a game of chance, in which each man fights and bets against fearful odds." [64] In October came his well-known letter to Henry James in which he said that after fifty years of optimistic content with civilization and the feeling that everything would come out all right in the end, he now felt that everything was coming out all wrong, and that America must base itself anew on real equality. "I should hardly like to trust pen and ink with the audacity of my social ideas," [65] he told James. Two weeks later he wrote Hale that he believed the present conditions of America were unjust, and that he did not think there was any real hope of justice under them. "I used to think America gave this [a fair chance to men]; now I don't." [66]

In 1888 also came *Annie Kilburn*. In this, the first of Howells' social novels, there is explicit praise of socialistic ideas. In the Reverend Peck's long sermon near the end of the book, the minister calls for human equality and for greater understanding between the industrial poor and the industrial rich. He believes that unwittingly trusts and monopolies "prophesy the end of competition" and "eliminate one element of strife, of rivalry, of warfare." [67] In a climactic passage he asks for a special kind of justice:

Not the justice of our Christless codes, with their penalties, but the instinct of righteous shame which, however dumbly, however obscurely, stirs in every honest man's heart when his superfluity is confronted with another's destitution and which is destined to increase in power till it becomes the social as well as the individual conscience. Then, in the truly Christian State, there shall be no more asking and no more giving, no more gratitude and no more merit, no more charity, but only and evermore justice; *all shall share alike, and want and luxury and killing toil and heartless indolence shall all cease together* [italics supplied].[68]

Thus 1888, the year of *Annie Kilburn* and the Howellses' settling in New York, was an all-important one. Tolstoy, the Haymarket aftermath, personal observation, strikes, violence, all combined to weld Howells' doubts of American *laissez faire* capitalism into a decisive firmness, and he believed some change of direction was imperative. The democrat of the Golden Age was now a modified socialist of the Industrial Age, and the leader of the American realistic school was ready to take on a new and more important task than any he had ever had before. He was ready to persuade America that acquisitive capitalism was not in keeping with its democratic and Christian traditions.

4

HOWELLS AND REFORM:

1888-1896

WITH THE PUBLICATION of *Annie Kilburn* and its concern for economic justice, Howells found himself in the middle of the growing agitation for reform. The 1880's and '90's became what Henry Steele Commager calls "something of a watershed" between the past and the present.[1] These years formed a line of demarcation between the old rural America and the new industrial America, and during these years the demand for economic reform became louder and more insistent. Not only were the ethical practices of capitalism condemned, but giant monopolies were recognized for the first time as threats to the worker, whose wages they could control in an oversupplied labor market, and to the middle-class businessman, who was often trapped into competing with the trusts or combining with them.

Moreover, the trend toward consolidation, begun after the Civil War, was quickened during the last decades of the century as the advantages of combination became obvious to wealthy industrialists. In 1880 there were 1,990 woolen mills in the

United States; in 1890 there were only 1,311, despite a growing demand for wool. In 1880 there were 1,934 agricultural implement factories in America; in 1890 only 910. Steel and iron mills decreased by a third and leather establishments by three-fourths.[2] The independent businessman, caught squarely between competition and combination, clamored for relief, and in 1890 Congress passed the Sherman Anti-Trust Act, a law which sought to limit activities of the larger combines. Three years earlier, western farmers and merchants, another middle-class group, had harried Congress into passing the Interstate Commerce Act, which laid the first restrictions on railroad pools and discriminatory rates.

Thus as the 1890's dawned, the middle-class protest against *laissez faire* capitalism was one of those most often heard. Monopoly, which seemed the natural culmination of industrial capitalism, deprived the little man of the livelihood and independence to which he was entitled under a democratic system. So reasoned many Americans who saw their own prospects and goals hampered by those of the trusts.

What course of action would best put the American system back in order? What changes were essential? Answers were abundant and varied. Henry George proposed a single tax on land which would take "the real source of wealth" from the hands of speculators and give it back to the people. E. L. Godkin argued for civil service reform and a more responsible plutocracy. Edward Bellamy sought a collectivization of society and a socialistic economic order. Robert Dale Owen advocated a system of industrial profit-sharing. Henry Lloyd wanted greater government intervention in the economic sphere. Andrew Carnegie spoke for more philanthropic action from those who benefited from free enterprise. Other solutions echoed back and forth across the country. From California to New England came plans and theories, some serious, some ridiculous.

As time passed it became clear that no one answer was completely acceptable. In fact, it soon became obvious that Tolstoy's pamphlet *Que Faire?* asked a question that had only begun to challenge Americans. William Dean Howells, for one, accepted the challenge eagerly. Once committed, he took up social problems with an alacrity that surprised and alarmed

many of his friends. After 1888, his column for *Harper's Monthly,*
the "Editor's Study," contained increasingly pointed social comment, and such comment continued until he left the post in
February 1892.[3] After that he kept up his analysis of society in
articles for *Scribner's, Century,* and the *North American Review.*

It is mainly, however, his novels of the period which reveal
the impact of the social crisis on his own thinking. For with the
exception of the second half of *Through the Eye of the Needle,*
written in 1907, all of Howells' social novels were finished between 1888 and 1893—*Annie Kilburn* in 1888, *A Hazard of New
Fortunes* in 1889, *The Quality of Mercy* in 1891, *A Traveler from
Altruria* in 1892, *The World of Chance* in 1892, and the first half
of *Through the Eye of the Needle* in 1893.[4] These books, along
with *Impressions and Experiences* (1896), a nonfiction work
primarily made up of articles published during this period, constitute Howells' best-known social criticism.

II

To understand this criticism, one must recognize that it has two
different bases—one philosophical and one humanitarian. On the
philosophical level Howells felt that *laissez faire* capitalism simply was not in keeping with a rational world order. From the
viewpoint of a man who accepted the rationalistic tradition of
the eighteenth century as Howells did, the idea of a government's or a society's refusing to regulate and adjust a dangerously
growing force in accordance with the best interests of the majority was criminal. To allow capitalism to take whatever form
it wished, to allow it to remain *laissez faire,* was to misunder-
stand both the universe and man's place in that universe.

Howells believed that the adherents of a totally free enterprise system overlooked two important facts about man's existence: one, that he was a rational animal and, two, that his
universe was understandable and significant. Howells felt that
man, by using his reason, could investigate the cosmos and
integrate himself and his institutions with an orderly natural
law. But the theory of *laissez faire,* letting things go on as they
came, could never bring man into the proper relationship with
a rational world order because man had no right to expect that
events naturally happened for the best.

It seemed obvious to Howells that some things did not bring improvement in either the short or long run. It was equally obvious that man must take a hand and mold his environment if he expected it to be reasonable. In *A Traveler from Altruria* and *Through the Eye of the Needle*, Howells describes a society that has decided on certain desirables and then systematically established them. Altruria has formed its environment to fit its needs; this idea Howells constantly emphasizes. But he felt that some capitalistic countries had consistently refused to consider the possibility of changing human conditions. Mrs. Eveleth Homos, writing from Altruria to Dolly Makely in America, says:

> They [Altrurian newspapers] . . . print selected passages of capitalistic history, from the earliest to the latest times, showing how in war and pestilence and needless disaster the world outside Altruria remains essentially the same that it was at the beginning of civilization, with some slight changes through the changes of human nature for the better in its slow approaches to the Altrurian ideal . . . the writers get sad amusement out of the fact that the capitalistic world believes human nature cannot be changed, though cannibalism and slavery and polygamy have all been extirpated in the so-called Christian countries.[5]

The concept of man's molding his environment owes much to Howells' early background in rural Ohio of 1840 and 1850 where, under the influence of the Enlightenment, such thinking was commonplace. But in taking such a view in 1890, Howells entered the lists in the major philosophical debate of the latter part of the nineteenth century: whether or not man could take an important role in his own destiny.

On one side, bolstered by Darwinian theories of evolutionary progress and the survival of the fittest, was a group of thinkers headed by Herbert Spencer and William Graham Sumner, who believed that man could make no significant contribution to the continuing advancement of the race. Man's duty, these writers held, was simply to keep his hands off the social condition and acquiesce in God's world. Progress had always been the result of natural law and would continue to be so. Man should attempt to adapt himself to his environment rather than try to change it—this was the theme of such works as Spencer's *Social Statics* and Sumner's "The Absurd Attempt to Make the World Over." Summer wrote:

> I must expect to be told here, according to the current fashions of thinking, that we ought to control the development of the organization of industry. The first instinct of modern man is to get a law passed to forbid or prevent what, in his wisdom, he disapproves. A thing which is inevitable, however, is one which we cannot control. We have to make up our minds to it, to adjust ourselves to it, and sit down to live with it . . . . The great stream of time and earthly things will sweep on just the same in spite of us. It bears with it now all the errors and follies of the past, the wreckage of all the philosophies. . . . It will absorb the efforts at change and take them into itself as new but trivial components, and the great movement of tradition and work will go on unchanged by our fads and schemes.[6]

With this emphasis Sumner and Spencer had an obvious appeal to the supporters of a traditional individualism and acquisitive capitalism.

Men like Lester Ward, the American sociologist, and John Wesley Powell, a noted geologist and expert on water resources, held contrary convictions. These men believed that the individual could and should control his environment. Science and investigation could combine to enable man to understand and control evolution, a process which went backward as well as forward. Nature herself was impartial and could in no way be considered responsible for progress. In fact, civilization always had been and would always be a triumph over the blind forces of nature, whether one dealt with social problems in New York or water problems in the arid West. Like Howells, these men believed that man, equipped with reason, could create a better society through the employment of that reason. Ward ends his *Dynamic Sociology*, whose title is a direct reply to Spencer's *Social Statics*, with these words:

> It is, in short, the question whether the social system shall always be left to nature, always be genetic and spontaneous, and be allowed to drift listlessly on, intrusted to the by no means always progressive influences which have developed it and

brought it to its present condition, or whether it shall be regarded as a proper subject of art, treated as other natural products have been treated by human intelligence and made as much superior to nature . . . as other artificial products are superior to natural ones.[7]

The lines of conflict were clear, and Howells in protesting against the lack of regulation of business found himself in a philosophical as well as a practical debate. Not only was the question "What is to be done?" being asked, but also the question "Should anything be done?" For Howells there might be several answers to the first, but there could be only one for the second—a clear, resounding "yes."

The reason for this answer was bound up with Howells' humanitarianism as well as with his philosophy. To Howells, the middle-class humanitarian ideals of equality, honesty, and fair dealing were being violated by the new materialism. He believed that the old equalitarian society with its idea of a larger life for the average man was disintegrating, and that the ideal of the millionaire had replaced that of the intellectual and well-rounded man. Now one sought money and position rather than knowledge and culture. Men no longer had time to read, or if they did, it was only to glance through the sensation-filled newspapers. Culture, civic responsibility, a sincere interest in politics were often forgotten. Because of these views, Howells looked dubiously at modern society:

I think it is something of a loss, that ebb of the high tide of political feeling which began with the era of our immense material prosperity. It was a feeling that formed the solidarity of all the citizens, and if it was not always, or often, the highest interest which can unite men, it was at least not that deadly and selfish cult of business which centres each of us in his own affairs and kills even our curiosity about others. Very likely people were less bent on the pursuit of wealth in those days because there was less chance to grow rich, but the fact remains that they were less bent in that direction, and that they gave their minds to other things more than they do now. I think those other things were larger things, and that our civic type was once nobler than it is. It was before the period of corruption, when it was not yet fully known that dollars can do the work of votes, when the votes as yet outnumbered the dollars, and more of us had the one than the other.[8]

III

As Howells saw it, a capitalistic society of rich and poor was degrading for both. For the poor it meant the slums, and a life of labor and debasement. In *A Hazard of New Fortunes,* Howells sketched briefly the wretchedness of poverty and tenement life in the character of Lindau, the old German who lived mostly on bread crusts and often stayed in bed all day to conserve his clothes, but it was in his article "An East-Side Ramble" (1896) that he painted his most detailed picture of the slums where living was "just short of the savage life." [9] Here he portrayed the ragged children, the stench, and the lack of sanitation that he found on a visit to New York's East Side. But more than with the physical decay, Howells was struck with the destruction of civilized values and particularly with the loss of human ambition. Many of the people were cheerful, to be sure, but as he walked among the Irish and Jews and Russians, he found a resignation and an acceptance of conditions that surprised him. These people were poor, and many of them felt they were always going to be poor. And in the end Howells was forced to agree with them.

> I could not see that in itself or in its condition it [the life of the poor] held the promise or the hope of anything better. If it is tolerable, it must endure; if it is intolerable, still it must endure. Here and there one will release himself from it, and doubtless numbers are always doing this, as in the days of slavery there were always fugitives, but for the great mass the captivity remains.[10]

"For the great mass the captivity remains." This was what bothered Howells. For here was a real paradox. America, the home of opportunity and, in Howells' eyes, the land of hope for the average man, was now actually condemning part of its population to a captivity of misery and hardship. Such captivity not only destroyed ethical values but kept man from fulfilling his human potential. It degraded the poor and deprived them of being what they might be. To Howells, this constituted human slavery as surely as that of the Negro in the antebellum South. He compared chattel and industrial slavery and found the latter more harmful and more damaging to American traditions.

In a real sense the wealthy suffered from unrestricted capitalism too, and Howells was able to give his portraits of the new millionaire a greater fullness than those of the exploited worker. The fullness in no way softens the description. It hardens it. Howells' picture of Dryfoos, the Ohio farmer in *A Hazard of New Fortunes* who became a millionaire after natural gas was discovered on his land, is a good example and reveals both the author's sympathy and his dislike. Basil March, Howells' spokesman, is speaking:

> I don't believe a man's any better for having made money so easily and rapidly as Dryfoos has done, and I doubt if he's any wiser . . . I guess he's come to despise a great many things that he once respected and that intellectual ability is among them— what *we* call intellectual ability. He must have undergone a moral deterioration, an atrophy of the generous instincts, and I don't see why it shouldn't have reached his mental make-up. He has sharpened, but he has narrowed; his sagacity has turned into suspicion, his caution to meanness, his courage to ferocity. That's the way I philosophize about a man of Dryfoos' experience and I am not very proud when I realize that such a man and his experience are the ideal and ambition of most Americans.[11]

This attitude toward the millionaire, this insistence on the moral and cultural limitations of men devoted exclusively to business, is a dominant characteristic in Howells' social novels. Such a characterization presents a picture of the man of wealth and business that was to have great vogue among later writers. Theodore Dreiser's Frank Cowperwood, Frank Norris' Curtis Jadwin, and Sinclair Lewis' George Babbitt, to mention only three fictional businessmen, have many of the same qualities that Howells pictured in his creations. Howells' portraits were not wholly original (Mark Twain and Charles Dudley Warner as early as 1869 in *The Gilded Age* had suggested some of the predatory qualities of American tycoons), but he was the first major writer in America to deal at some length with the successful man of business. His Gerrishes, his Dryfooses, his Northwicks, all have traits which were to be copied later.

The most pitiful of Howells' businessmen is John Milton Northwick (his author must have chuckled at the name), the successful financier in *The Quality of Mercy*. Here Howells draws a character virtually devoid of any talent but that of making money. Northwick has no intellectual curiosity, no cultivation whatsoever. He has no interests, no hobbies, no enthusiasms. After he has defalcated to Canada with company funds and is forced to spend a winter in icebound Haha Bay, he is worthless as a companion to the friendly trapper, Bird, and the French priest, Father Etiènne. These two sound him on almost every possible subject but find him only narrow and ignorant. He cares little for nature and nothing for art; he does not read or show any liking for music. He has no interest in ethics or politics or science. Finally the young priest perceived

> that his gentlemanly decorum and grave repose of manner masked a complete ignorance of the things that interest cultivated people, and that he was merely and purely a business man, a figment of commercial civilization, with only the crudest tastes and ambitions outside of the narrow circle of making money. . . . It was only when Pere Etiènne gave him up as the creature of a civilization too ugly and too arid to be borne, that he began to love him as a brother.[12]

In the Northwick family, Howells pictures in miniature the transition from America of the Golden Age to that of the Gilded Age. The businessman's father was a typical American of the earlier day. He ran a drug and book store in a small New England village and "cared more for the literary than the pharmaceutical side of it; he liked to have a circle of cronies about the wood-stove in his store till midnight, and discuss morals and religion with them. . . ."[13] His son, however, after some early education at home, married a wealthy woman and turned to the best avenue for fame and position—business. The father and son grew steadily apart, and at the time of the story they do not visit each other.

> The elder Northwick used sometimes to speak of his son and his success in the world not boastfully, but with a certain sarcasm for the source of his bounty, as a boy who had always disappointed him by a narrowness of ambition. He called him Milt, and he said he supposed now Milt was the most self-satisfied man in Massachusetts; he implied that there were better things than material success.[14]

Howells did a great deal more than imply.

I V

For Howells, not only did the rich and the poor suffer from unrestricted capitalism, but the social climate itself was vitally affected. Any philosophy that allowed a virtual warfare to elevate a few and depress the many created an unhealthful environment for all. It created a grab-and-get philosophy which affected merchants, farmers, teachers, doctors, lawyers—as well as millionaires and workers. Success and money became the supreme goals, and one reached them the best way he could.

Howells' consciousness of the influence of environmental forces on social behavior first appears in his writings around 1886. His basic premise had always been and was always to be that the individual was personally responsible for his actions. This is as true in *The Leatherwood God* in 1916 as it is in *Silas Lapham* in 1884. But Howells began to see that man did not make decisions in a vacuum and that it took bravery and intelligence to resist social forces. He first broaches these ideas in *The Minister's Charge* (1886) when Mr. Sewell in his climactic sermon says that no man's sin affects himself alone and that society has a part in evil by setting up false goals and not stamping out discernible wrongs.[15]

The most complete treatment, however, occurs in *The Quality of Mercy* (1891). Here Howells does an interesting thing. He looks at Northwick's defalcation from two points of view— Northwick's and that of certain townspeople. In Northwick's mind there is no doubt of his own guilt. He realizes it throughout, and at the end longs for expiation in the symbol of the handcuffs which he asks Pinney to put on him. But from the outsider's viewpoint, Howells emphasizes the role that society played in the crime. Putney, the perceptive small-town lawyer, is emphatic in his belief that social pressures had produced a kind of insanity in Northwick which in turn brought on his crime.* Maxwell's editorial on Northwick also puts a great deal of the blame on society and on "the struggle for money going on around us." The young writer remarks that "it behooved society to consider how far it was itself responsible, which it might well do without ignoring the responsibility of the criminal." [16] And Putney succinctly sums up Howells' feelings at the end. "He [Northwick] just seems to be a kind of—incident; and a pretty common kind. He was a mere creature of circumstances —like the rest of us. His environment made him rich, and his environment made him a rogue." [17]

Here Howells reveals a definite inclination toward the determinism of the naturalists. He was turning with his times and, though he expressed his dislike of the philosophy of Zola and Hardy and the brutalization of life which might result from such a view, he allowed similar ideas to come into his own work. His observation of society and his reading of the naturalists probably combined in making him increasingly aware of the influence of environmental forces in shaping man's behavior. He criticized George Eliot in 1894 because of "the undue burden she seems to throw upon the individual, and her failure to account largely enough for motive from the social environment." [18]

Howells, however, could not go all the way in putting the entire blame for crime or evil on the environment. Man maintained some control over, and thus some responsibility for, his

---

* See Putney's comments, *The Quality of Mercy*, 454. That all criminals were in some sense insane and thus not responsible for their acts was a Swedenborgian doctrine that Howells first learned from his father, a staunch supporter of the Swedish theologian. Howells mentions the doctrine in several places and discusses it briefly in his essay, "I Talk of Dreams," *Harper's Monthly*, XC (May 1895), 836-845. His thinking here seems to have been that there was much in the idea, although he apparently did not realize the implication of such a doctrine on his conviction that man bore personal responsibility for his actions.

own acts—of this Howells was sure. Both the reader and North-wick are clearly mindful of the latter's guilt, and nothing in Howells' later social novels ever shows a change in this thinking. But the significant point here is that Howells did not under-estimate the influence of environment on man. He realized that when social conditions became corrupt, men usually suffered the same fate. Though he was not one of the naturalists, he saw a partial truth in their doctrine.

Howells' indictment of capitalistic society was a complete one. He believed that such a society hurt the rich, the poor, the mid-dle class, and the total environment. He believed that this dam-age was a perversion of what social intercourse should be. To a man of the Golden Age, society, the medium of interchange between people and ideas, was the chief civilizing force in any culture. It was society's function to round off man's rough spots, erase the primitive and brutal in him, and make him stronger and more able to live in a civilized world. Dr. Olney, the hero of *An Imperative Duty*, remarks:

> The tame man, the civilized man, is stronger than the wild man; and . . . where there are very strong ancestral procliv-ities on one side especially toward evil, they will die out before the good tendencies on the other side, for much the same rea-son, that is, vice is savage and virtue is civilized.[19]

The banker in *A Traveler from Altruria* comments:

> We may laugh at the emptiness of society, or pretend to be sick of it, but there is no doubt that society is the flower of civilization and to be shut out from it is to be denied the best privileges of a civilized man.[20]

It was because of this view of the civilizing function of society that Howells was so seriously disturbed by the social results of capitalism.

V

The problem of social influence bothered Howells so much that he spent a great deal of effort in both his Utopian romances describing the environment in Altruria. Here there was no money

or emphasis on material possessions. Man was placed in circumstances that would bring out his natural talents and help him
acquire new ones.[21] He lived in a classless society, had ample
time for education and the arts, enjoyed economic security,
shared his work and experiences with his neighbors. But in a
capitalistic culture, such conditions were impossible. Class divisions were inevitable, and with such divisions, neither men
nor societies could attain their highest potential. Here one sees
Howells' old-time equalitarianism. He believed, much as Tolstoy
did, that people knew and understood each other only if they
were in some way socially equal and their lives and circumstances were similar. Human sympathy, he felt, could spring
only from shared feelings. The rich, by rising above work and
need, and by cutting themselves off from common experiences,
were growing away from the poor and the middle class. Such
division resulted in self-centeredness and lack of communication
between groups.

Howells treats this theme of division many times in his novels
—in *Annie Kilburn, The Minister's Charge, A Hazard of New
Fortunes,* and *A Traveler from Altruria.*[22] All deal with the
problems inherent in a class society, a society Howells felt
America had not known before. Usually the central problem is
the same; how can one establish love and free interchange between the rich and the poor if their circumstances have nothing
in common? Howells considers and rejects personal charity,
though he feels it may create a bond of gratitude.[23] What is
needed is a feeling of human sympathy which can only spring
from likeness. The Reverend Peck says in *Annie Kilburn:*

> In the political world we have striven forward to liberty as to
> the final good, but with this achieved we find that liberty is only
> a means and not an end, and that we shall abuse it as a means
> if we do not use it, even to sacrifice it, to promote equality, or
> in other words, equality is the perfect work, the evolution of
> liberty.[24]

This equality was a kind of social inclusion which was to ex-
tend not only to the rich and the poor but to all races as well.
In the one novel where Howells touches on the question of the
Negro in society, *An Imperative Duty,* Olney, the hero and a

stout defender of the Negroes, affirms their right to social equality. The Negroes' rejection by their fellowmen, he says, "strikes me as one of the most preposterous, the most monstrous things in the world."[25] One need not intermarry with them, he remarks, "but short of that I don't see why one shouldn't associate with them."[26]

> . . . we might recognize them as fellow-beings in public, if we don't in private; but we ignore, if we don't repulse them at every point—from our business as well as our bosoms. Yes, it strikes one as very odd . . . very funny, very painful.[27]

Christian equality, Howells points out, is the natural right of all citizens in America.[*]

But despite Howells' belief that social equality, social inclusion, was the ultimate answer to class division, he saw that what had served as the basis for equality in the earlier Midwest, the agrarian-rural pattern of life, was gone. What Mr. Homos calls "the purer age" had disappeared, and Howells realized that the past was not recallable. Nonetheless he was pensive. He believed the earlier days were better for society because they gave men a chance for greater achievement. And here was Howells' basic stricture against a class society—*it did not permit the fullest development of the group.* In fact, it created vices. He wrote:

> Is the arrest of development greater on the plain of society than on its summits or in its abysses? . . . Have the inventions, the good books, the beautiful pictures and statues, the just laws, the animal comforts even, come from the uppermost or the lower-most classes? They have mostly come from the middle classes . . . from the inexhaustible and generous vitality of the widest level of life . . . . Inequality still persists, but so does murder, so does unchastity, so do almost all the sins and shames that ever were. Inequality is, in fact, the sum of them; in this body of death they fester and corrupt forever. As long as we have

---

[*] Howells felt about immigrants as he felt about Negroes. His article, "Our Italian Assimilators" (*Harper's Weekly*, LIII [April 10, 1909], 28), implicitly asks for the social equality of all races in America. Mr. Peck in his sermon in *Annie Kilburn* also echoes this point. See *Annie Kilburn*, 239, 240.

inequality we shall have these sins and shames which spring from it, and which live on from inferior to superior. Few vices live from equal to equal; but the virtues flourish.[28]

Thus, as with the individual, society benefited when man-made distinctions were eliminated. Howells readily admitted that natural inequalities would always exist.[29] They were not controllable by man. Artificial inequalities, however, were, and if a system could be found that would eliminate class distinctions and guarantee a modicum of social equality, America might reverse the trend toward a stratified society and revive the dream of a better life for the common man. The theory of *laissez faire* capitalism obviously would not do. This was apparent to Howells from the beginning. Capitalism only strengthened the barriers between men and intensified the struggle to get ahead. It produced the Gerrishes, the Dryfooses, and the Northwicks among the rich, and the Lindaus, the Camps, and the Dentons among the poor. It pitted one man against another and told them to fight it out. Basil March comments on the capitalistic society in *A Hazard of New Fortunes:*

> Someone always has you by the throat, unless you have someone else in *your* grip. I wonder if that's the attitude the Almighty intended his respectable creatures to take toward one another . . . we go on, pushing and pulling, climbing and crawling, thrusting aside and trampling underfoot, lying, cheating, stealing; and when we get to the end, covered with blood and dirt and sin and shame, and look back over the way we've come . . . I don't think the retrospect can be pleasing.[30]

On the other hand, Howells thought that cooperation might be the answer:

> The millennium, the reign of Christliness on earth, will be nothing mystical or strange. It will be the application of a very simple rule [human cooperation] to life, which we find in no wise difficult or surprising where the economic conditions do not hinder its operation. The members of a family live for one another as unconsciously as they live upon all others. There is no effort, no friction in their perpetual surrender of their several

interests to the common good; and in the state there need really be none, if once the needs of livelihood were assured to every citizen.[31]

In this manner Howells turns to cooperation, to his concept of socialism, for fulfillment of human potential. But it is important to note that Howells' criticism of capitalism was almost wholly moral and humanistic. It was not basically economic. He did believe socialism would prove more efficient than capitalism,[32] but this was not his main consideration. It was enough for Howells that capitalism deprived men of a fundamental right to enlightenment and a full personal life. This belief was to have important consequences when Howells constructed his ideal society. In the Altrurian romances, works less economically oriented than those of Bellamy or George, Howells attacked the problems arising from industrialism by presenting solutions which were primarily ethical. He was more interested in describing a rural environment where one read and had an opportunity for personal fulfillment than he was in depicting the role that machines played in such an economy or the methods of production and distribution. Money or the system of commercial exchange is hardly discussed at all, but the cultural and ethical advantages of village life receive attention throughout both books. Because of this emphasis, many modern students of economics have dismissed Howells as a man who meant well but had nothing to offer in the way of reform. Yet to ask for a complete economic program in the Altrurian novels is to require from Howells something that he did not require from himself and to misconstrue what he did write. Such an attitude can lead, and indeed has led, to a misunderstanding of his work.[33]

One other point should be emphasized here. William Dean Howells was not an economist. He had no training in economic theory and knew of the subject only what he had read from such writers as Laurence Gronlund, Richard T. Ely, and Edward Atkinson.* He knew neither the classical economists, Smith,

---

* These men were contemporary economists whose works were known to Howells. Atkinson, the author of several articles for the *Atlantic* during Howells' editorship, was an industrialist and economist who, though a conservative, had some liberal ideas concerning labor and agriculture. Ely, an economics professor at Johns Hopkins and Wisconsin, was the author

Ricardo, Malthus, nor the more contemporary theorists such as Marx or Engels. He knew little about taxation, supply, or production methods. He was in reality an intellectual amateur, the product of an earlier America, in a field which was rapidly becoming specialized.

In addition to this lack of specialized knowledge, Howells' economics often contains a vagueness that is disturbing. Critics who read only the Altrurian romances might agree with Hartley Grattan that Howells was a "garden party socialist." [34] Howells' ideal conditions sometimes appear without the author's having explained how they originate; in places he avoids the fundamental question of how Utopia is brought into being. Moreover, some of his suggestions have little if any practical value. They represent personal whims and at times obscure more important ideas. Yet even with these reservations, one finds in Howells a provocativeness and perception that make his social writings well worth study. Like Thoreau, Howells was beginning to nibble at the wrong end of the asparagus, and this process brought new ideas and attitudes.

---

of several books which advocated greater governmental intervention in economic matters. Gronlund was one of the best-known American socialists in the 1880's and '90's and the author of *The Cooperative Commonwealth,* a book which sought to adapt Marxian ideas to the American environment.

5

SOCIAL COMMENTARY

O N THE THEORETIC LEVEL, the basis of all Howells' reform lay in economic security. Without this Howells felt there could be no permanent progression toward a productive, democratic state. He held that all civil liberties, including the right to vote, were shams unless there was also economic security. In "The Nature of Liberty" (1895), he comments:

> Till a man is economically independent, he is not free. . . .
> He may have the right to speak freely, print freely, pray freely, vote freely; but he cannot manfully use his right, though warranted in it by the constitutions and the statutes of all the States, if he is afraid another man may take away his means of livelihood for doing so.[1]

Earlier in the same essay he defines liberty as an entity based on "security from want and the fear of want."[2] This concept is fundamental in Howells' socialism, which became for him the system by which a government can best provide a man with a job and thus in a measure guarantee economic security. "Liberty and poverty are incompatible," Howells writes, and only by destroying poverty can a country really be free.[3]

Of course Howells realized that opportunity was a part of liberty too, but he saw it as a secondary part:

> If we wished to keep liberty simply as opportunity, we should lose it, for there is nothing vital, nothing lasting in opportunity. We can enjoy liberty only in its ultimate form of safety, and we cannot any of us . . . be safe unless all the rest are safe, for the insecurity of others is the perpetual menace of our own security.[4]

But economic security was not the final end. It was only a means to economic equality. Here Howells enters into difficulties. For the economic equality that he was seeking, a kind of industrial parallel to the Western equalitarianism he had known in his youth, would seem possible only in a socialistic system, as indeed he pictures it in the Altrurian romances. Yet Howells also tries to imagine it in capitalistic conditions. In one of the most idealistic articles he ever wrote, "Equality as the Basis of Good Society" (1895), he attempts to show that polite society where the high and low meet in friendly equality may serve as the model for a classless group in the future. Good society is expanding, he thinks, and the new equality will come when that society embraces all mankind:

> As nearly as we can conceive it or forecast it, the new condition, the equality of the future, will be the enlargement of good society to the whole of humanity. This seems to me so not only because, so far as we have social equality, it has grown out of human nature, but because we have already more of that equality than any other.[*]

---

[*] Howells, *Century*, XXIX, 67. This idea contradicts Howells' thinking on society as expressed in *Annie Kilburn* and *A Hazard of New Fortunes* where he feels that the division into classes is narrowing and constricting society in a way previously unknown in America. In "Equality as the Basis of Good Society," he sees good (high) society, whose lack of rapport with the rest of the classes had caused some of the division, as a friendly, expanding entity which may bring about social equality.

The objections here are obvious. Good society seldom really included any of the low to begin with, it was not always friendly, and the principles of affable equality have not always been carried over into business or modern life in general. The point here, however, is that Howells tried to visualize social equality in a capitalistic system. His equality seems based on good fellowship, courtesy, and a recognition of other men's worth, qualities which seem out of character with the *laissez faire* system which Howells himself often criticized.

Later in the article Howells changes his position. He writes that "economic equality is the mother of all other equalities" and that from it grow political, judicial, and social equality.[5] Now man's equalness is not based on a kind of *bonhomie* but on the consideration that all men work and that they receive a similar compensation for their work. Howells seems to recognize his inconsistency, for he immediately adds that though there are financial differences in America, "money means less in good society than elsewhere," and thus good society is better able to approach social equality.[6] Yet he seems unable to avoid the awkward position of saying that true equality must come through economic equality, and that it *might* also come through good society where there are money differences. The two statements are antithetical because in the second he presupposes capitalistic conditions where there are gradations of income and in the first, socialistic conditions where there are no, or only slight, gradations. He is working with two different ideas without seeing a fundamental conflict between the two.

But if Howells is confused here, he is not usually so. Other writings show a more definite stand. In the article "Who Are Our Brethren?" (1896), he emphasizes the idea that economic equality is the basis of social equality. Only when economic equality is established can men begin to give each other the understanding which comes from "common experience and mutual knowledge, from common aspiration and endeavor."[7] This is essentially the same point that the Reverend Peck makes in *Annie Kilburn* when he says that "sympathy—common feeling—the sense of fraternity—can spring only from like experiences, like hopes, like fears," and that a class society of workers and leisured rich eliminates such a rapport between men.[8] Without some semblance of economic equality, Peck believes that there can be no identification between men, which is "the only rest and comfort and pleasure that men can know." [9]

In *Annie Kilburn*, the novelist forgets about the idea of equality's materializing through society and emphasizes its coming through economic parity. It will emerge, he feels, through an arrangement by which some financial similarity is assured. But even here Howells is not always clear. Nowhere, for example, does he really define what he means by the term "economic equality." Does he mean similar jobs and similar compensations as in Altruria, or does he mean equality within certain specified limits of income, or does he use the term as a synonym for economic security as he implies at times in "The Nature of Liberty"? [10]

Moreover, Howells is not always consistent in explaining how such economic equality originates. It comes, of course, through some kind of socialistic process, but Howells never seems completely satisfied with the method. For a while he believes that economic equality will come when the government takes over the one big monopoly into which all business appears irresistibly headed. This idea was a favorite one with the socialists, and Howells uses it both in *Annie Kilburn* (1888), where the Reverend Peck hints at its success,[11] and in *A Traveler from Altruria* (1895), where it actually is the process by which Altruria becomes a socialistic state.[12]

But though he accepted the idea, Howells seems to have had his doubts of it. In *The World of Chance* (1892), a German socialist openly disavows the concept and remarks, "As far back as Louis Napoleon's rise we have been expecting the growth of the corporate industries to accomplish our purposes for us. But between the corporation and collectivity there is a gulf—a chasm that has never yet been passed." [13] Hughes, Howells' spokesman, disagrees with this point of view, but there seems to be a real question in Howells' mind, for after 1893 he is never explicit on exactly how socialism and economic equality come into being. After the turn of the century and the beginning of the trust-busting activities of Theodore Roosevelt, the idea seems forgotten altogether. It is significantly omitted in the second part of *Through the Eye of the Needle* written in 1907. But even before this, in 1895, Howells tells his readers that the method of change from inequality may be unknown at present.

> Perhaps we shall be changed by the slow process of the years, and by a process no more visible in the present than the movement of the hand upon the clock, but destined to a greater and greater swiftness in the future.[14]

It is this problem of economic equality that Howells is never quite able to solve. He is never able to picture it clearly for the reader. Probably it was unclear in his own mind; at any rate the ideal today still seems as vague as it did when Howells first conceived it in the 1880's. The idea, however, does not mean that Howells believed a *wholly* equal society would result from economic parity. He saw plainly that there were educational, physical, and mental differences between men that would never allow them to enjoy exactly the same status;[15] but he did believe that economic parity could help erase the *artificial* distinctions between men and thus give society a greater inclusiveness and unity. As we have seen, such unity was tremendously important to Howells. He felt that both individuals and groups gained in maturity and understanding by wide contact with people. The best cider came from a mixed crush of apples, and in the same way the best democracy came from the vitality and brotherhood of equality.[16]

Howells' lesser goal, economic security, has been more important in American history than the concept of economic parity. Through the years the idea that government has some responsibility for the economic well-being of its people has slowly gained acceptance and now in various forms is generally regarded as feasible and proper. Paradoxically, however, it was this idea of economic security which caused Howells the most anguish during the early '90's. He believed that in a democracy the people were their own masters and had only to vote into effect any desired change. To him some proposed legislation was obviously good for the lower and middle classes, which controlled the majority of votes. Yet such plans were never voted into law. Howells asked why. The more he thought about the matter, the more he came to the conclusion that one restraining factor outweighed all others—human selfishness. The poor and the struggling were unwilling to vote for any laws which some day might rob them of their chance to be wealthy and powerful. Opportunity and one view of Americanism had been indissolubly linked, and Howells felt that many Americans wanted to rise, even at the expense of their fellows. He continually hammered at this kind of thinking. In 1894 he told his readers:

> Any other sort of wage-taker [than a socialist] is ready at the first chance to become a wage-giver, and to prosper as far as he can upon a margin in the value of the thing he gets someone else to make beyond the wage he gives for making it; and with this hope in his heart, he is as thoroughly a plutocrat as any present millionaire. . . . In fact, if we have ceased to be a democracy and have become a plutocracy, it is because the immense majority of the American people have no god before Mammon.[17]

Viewing the same dichotomy that de Tocqueville had noted some sixty years before—the parallel traditions of individualism and cooperation—Howells believed that Americans were choosing individualism at the very time when cooperation was so needed, when cooperation could give some kind of security. Because they were greedy, or rather because their circumstances made them greedy, people had embraced an evil rather than a good. Howells could only be dismayed and tell his readers frankly where the responsibility for improvement lay:

> If the poor American does not like it [the fact that money-making is the supreme American ideal], or if he does not prefer a plutocracy to a democracy, he has the affair in his own hands, for he has an overwhelming majority of the votes. At the end, as in the beginning, it is he who is responsible, and if he thinks himself unfairly used, it is he who ultimately makes and unmakes the laws, by political methods which, if still somewhat clumsy, he can promptly improve. It is time, in fine, that he should leave off railing at the rich, who . . . are infinitely fewer than the poor, and have but one vote apiece, unless the poor sell them more. If we have a plutocracy, it may be partly because the rich want it, but it is infinitely more because the poor choose it or allow it.[18]

II

Inextricably related to Howells' ideas on security and equality are those on socialism. Here, as in his criticism of capitalism, Howells implies the possibility of eventually establishing a near-perfect society. "The kingdom of God on earth," says the minister in *A Traveler from Altruria,* "it ought not to be incredible . . ."; [19] and it is not, the Altrurian returns, if men are brought up in the proper environment—an environment that men are capable of establishing.[20]

Here and elsewhere, Howells shows a basic optimism. He believes that the rational tendency of men is toward orderliness and integration into a beneficent world order. Theoretically at least, there was no reason why men should not progress and ultimately reach a kind of millennium on earth. In his article "Who Are Our Brethren?" (1896), Howells writes that men can work toward and achieve such an ideal goal if they apply reason and effort to the task. But they must work for this goal; it will not come to them automatically as Spencer or Sumner would have him believe. "We shall not have fraternity, human brotherhood without trying for it. From nature, it did not come; it came from the heart of man, who in the midst of nature is above it." [21]

In the Altrurian stories Howells depicted America in the first half of the books and Altruria in the second half. In the latter sections he described his ideal commonwealth, and it is not surprising that Altruria should strongly resemble the antebellum West that Howells knew as a boy. His socialism is essentially a barn-raising, housewarming kind of cooperation between rural neighbors. In Altruria most of the people live in small country towns of ten or twelve families. During the three-hour obligatory work periods they plant or reap in the fields or work at other village occupations. During harvest the men work in groups gathering the crops at one farm, then at another. The women do their housekeeping cooperatively, caring for one another's homes during illnesses. Since the villages are almost in sight of each other, there is a great deal of intermingling between groups during both the obligatory and the voluntary hours, when one may do as he wishes. Most entertainment occurs in the village, where the younger people sing and dance and act in plays while the older men and women talk, read, or pursue hobbies. There are some machines in Altruria—electric trains, motor boats, automobiles—but they are all publicly owned and are used primarily in the larger cities to facilitate travel. When a man loses his job because of a machine, he is put to work on a public project until some arrangements can be made for his employment. The headquarters for such projects are in the cities, which also house administrative offices, food centers, and museums where art and musical festivals are held. The people visit there often but are always happy to return to the country and their farms. Mrs. Homos writes:

> The earth is dear to them because they get their life from it by labor that is not slavery; they come to love very acre, every foot because they have known it from childhood; and I have seen old men, very old, pottering around the orchards and meadows during the hours of voluntary work, and trimming them up here and there, simply because they could not keep away from the place, or keep their hands off the trees and bushes.[22]

With this love of the rural life and their attempts at self-betterment through study and reading, the Altrurians closely resemble the Jeffersonian agrarians.

Politically, Altruria is a thoroughgoing democracy. The women enjoy complete political equality with the men. (When *A Traveler from Altruria* was written in 1892, only two states had granted full political rights to women.) They vote with the men and have full privileges in the large townhall-like meetings in which all important issues are discussed before a vote is taken. The government itself is run by elected and appointed officials who control all phases of production and distribution and who are instantly responsible to the voters. All changes are voted into law, and Howells emphasizes the fact that the Altrurians have attained their socialism by evolutionary, not revolutionary, means. Legal procedure is scrupulously followed, and violence is virtually unknown. Historically, America and Altruria have followed identical paths of political development; both have been monarchies, republics, states of "accumulation capitalism."

They differ only in that Altruria has taken the final step into socialism, a step that allows Howells opportunity for comment and satire.

Political equality, however, is only the means to a greater end—social equality. Every aspect of life in Altruria is organized to insure the greatest degree of social equality for all its citizens. There are no classes in society, and everyone shares equally in the economic prosperity or depression of the country. Depressions are extremely rare, however, because public ownership has proved so much more efficient than private. There is no money in Altruria, and everyone must buy his way with work. All purchasing of food and other essentials is done by a work-card which is validated only after the owner has fulfilled his obligatory work periods. Families are encouraged to eat together in the village communal dining halls, and usually do so, though they may dine privately if they wish. Entertainment, however, springs from the community, and the singing, fellowship, and conversation that follow meals constitute real sources of pleasure. Families are usually small, with no more than three children, and the parents, relieved of business pressures, are able to devote a great deal of time to their children. The mother and father are held strictly accountable for any delinquency of their children and for acquainting them with the traditions of Altruria. The schools help in these respects, and a love of country and its customs is not hard to develop, particularly after the children compare Altruria with capitalistic countries.

The guiding principle of Altruria is duty towards others. The traditional belief is that citizens have responsibilities to their neighbors and that these take precedence over their own rights. Capital punishment is outlawed, and the remorse that accompanies a crime is considered punishment enough under Altrurian conditions. Work is the ideal, and an object that is "honest and useful" is beautiful. To the esthetically minded Altrurians, the poet or artist is usually the most admired type because through his art or literature he brings the greatest happiness to the greatest number.

Yet some of the means by which this near-perfect society is reached are never completely clear. In both *A Traveler from Altruria* and *Through the Eye of the Needle* Howells simply wishes away some difficulties facing contemporary society. There are, for instance, no wars in Altruria because the entire nation donned arms the one time war did threaten and so cowed the enemy that he immediately sued for peace.[23] There are no religious dissensions, or even different denominations, because all citizens believe in Christ and look to His life for guidance rather than to dogmas that have grown up around His life.[24] There are no industrial cities because people have come to realize that rural life is more satisfying and healthful.[25] As to practical suggestions on how to establish these new conditions, Howells is silent. He is more interested in their effect on man and society than in their origin. Since wars, cities, and religious controversies hamper men in attaining freedom and a better life, they have no place in Howells' Utopia.

Yet the fact that Howells often does not concern himself with the realistic aspects of problems suggests the spirit in which the stories were written. Both books are dreams, fantasies, romances, where the writer is allowed the full scope of his imagination in visualizing the ideal state. Howells was simply following the lead of Plato and Sir Thomas More and such contemporary writers as Edward Bellamy and William Morris. The latter two made the Utopian novel extremely popular in the 1880's and '90's and used it as a vehicle of economic reform, permitting themselves a wide range in contrasting the real with the ideal.*

---

* Vernon L. Parrington, Jr., in his book *American Dreams*, lists forty Utopian novels written in the United States between 1880 and 1900. Most of these follow the pattern of Edward Bellamy's *Looking Backward* (1886) in comparing the present with a scientific Utopia of the future. For example, Bellamy pictures an urbanized society in which the machine has given man domination over nature. Men and women have obligatory tasks at certain ages, and work schedules and home life are regulated to allow for labor and leisure. On the whole, the State acts as a benevolent despot insuring abundance, providing education, and encouraging creative art and a higher spiritual life. Howells' books, on the other hand, look back to the rural, less mechanized past where country life constituted the ideal. The majority of the people are farmers and handicraft workers who live in small villages. Only essential machines are employed; play and recreation are largely spontaneous; and the family is the important unit. There is less emphasis on the State (though it controls production and distribution) and the less hurried, community-centered life serves as the model to compare with the present.

Altrurian conditions were as close as Howells could come to perfection, and he did not always trouble himself with probabilities.

Even perfection has its blemishes, however, and Howells had doubts and misgivings about aspects of Altruria. In an illuminating letter to Charles Eliot Norton, he wrote:

> Then in the midst of all, I have given my own dream of Utopia, which I fancy your not liking, unless for its confessions of imperfections even in Utopia. All other dreamers of such dreams have nothing but pleasure in them; I have had touches of nightmare.[26]

Though Howells never specifically mentions what touches of nightmare bothered him, the inevitable regimentation that accompanies cooperation may have disturbed him. Nevertheless many of the suggestions were to be taken seriously—using the vote to establish the cooperative state, abolishing capital punishment, lowering class barriers, promoting a love of home and work. Just as obviously, many of them were not. Howells was well aware that all-vegetable diets (he hated to see animals killed for food), regulations for uniform dress, religious unity, and an industrial system based on village crafts were personal ideals impossible to attain. There is in both books a curious mixture of practicality and idealism, and this, along with a sketchiness, a hit-and-run technique, a refusal to penetrate deeply into the consequences of his ideas, damages the two novels as social commentaries. Critics who find the Altrurian stories trivial and indict the author as unwilling to deal with significant issues are in danger of throwing the baby out with the bath.[27] There is, however, no denying that Howells' serious reforms are inadequately presented in the books and that one must go beyond them in order to get a full view of his thinking.

III

With all his idealism and desire for an unattainable past, Howells was a practical American, and many of his reforms should be regarded as practical measures. He called himself a "secular socialist" in contrast to a monastic or revolutionary socialist.

"Secular socialists choose to remain in the world and socialize it by franchise, and by the gradual extension of the popular owner-ship to the things they believe naturally common," he wrote in 1895.[28]

Howells chose secularism after careful consideration of the other forms. Revolutionism, he concluded, was wrong because it proposed to bring about the millennium in the wrong way. With his Quaker background, Howells grew to hate industrial violence and could never accept its use in establishing the new society. "Every drop of blood shed for a good cause helps to make it a bad cause," he wrote his father in 1892,[29] and each instance of violence creates a "bloodmist through which the situation shows wrong." [30] Physical force not only was morally wrong, it hurt the cause. The banker in A Traveler from Altruria says:

> How do they [the workers] go about to better themselves? They strike. Well a strike is a fight, and in a fight now-a-days, it is always skill and money that win. The workingmen can't stop till they put themselves outside of the public sympathy which the newspapers say is so potent in their behalf. . . . They destroy property and they interfere with business—the two absolutely sacred things in the American religion.[31]

If revolution was not the right course, neither was monastic socialism. By retiring from society, socialists took themselves and their ideas out of circulation and influence. Moreover, they eventually had to become a party to competitive conditions, whether they wished to or not. Howells writes:

> Hawthorne finds some pensive amusement in the fact that at Blithedale the brotherhood which intended the reign of peace and good will in the economic world must needs do its best or its worst to undersell and overreach the neighboring farmers in the markets, quite in the old wicked way; and this is always the obstacle that blocks the wheels of the one-horse millenium.[32]

It was only by remaining in the world that one could help society, and as Howells watched society in the late 1880's and early '90's, he was certain some help was imperative. In 1894, during strikes and hard times, the quiet, gray little man, whom many people then and since have called mild and reticent, boiled over with indigation:

> The tramps walk the land like the squalid spectres of the laborers who once tilled it. The miners have swarmed up out of their pits, to starve in the open air. In our paradise of toil, myriads of workingmen want work; the water is shut off in the factory, the fires are cold in the foundry. The public domain, where in some sort the poor might have provided for themselves, has been lavished on corporations, and its millions of acres have melted away as if they had been a like area of summer clouds.
>
> It is true that we still have the trusts, the syndicates, the combinations of roads, mines, and markets, the whole apparatus. If there is much cold and hunger, the price of food and fuel is yet so high as to afford a margin to the operators in coal and grain and meat. The great fortunes in almost undiminished splendor, remain the monuments of a victory that would otherwise look a good deal like defeat, and they will be an incentive to the young in the hour of our returning prosperity.[33]

Then in irony he adds, "We must not shut our eyes to the gain because it involves a great deal of loss." [34]

With a bitter heart Howells turned to practical reform. Perhaps the most socialistic of all his proposals was the one he shared with the Populists—the nationalization of so-called natural monopolies. Railroads, express lines, telegraph lines, gas and water works, and later telephone and electric power circuits—these were all natural monopolies because they were areas where competition was impractical. With the Populists, Howells believed that public control of these monopolies would correct injustices in high rates, poor service, and other discriminatory practices which some companies had foisted on the public because of their exclusive control. He felt that the management of these industries would provide the starting point for common ownership of all means of production and distribution. In his Altruria, the golden age begins when the government takes over the telegraph lines. The people then gain control of the express business, the railroads, and eventually all means of transportation.[35] In The World of Chance, Hughes, the old socialist

and an auctorial voice, remarks that the first step in building
a strong socialistic system is the management of such natural
monopolies as the telegraphs, the railroads, and the expresses.[36]

Another suggestion was the preservation of the public domain.
Like the followers of Henry George, Howells saw that the railroads and real estate speculators had gobbled up huge chunks
of Western farm lands that had formerly been conceived of
as an escape valve for the poor and struggling. Whether these
lands ever served such a purpose has been seriously questioned
in modern times,[37] but there is no doubt that the intent of the
Homestead Act (1862) was not only to encourage settlement of
the West but to provide those in financial difficulty with the
means for a new start. Under the terms of the act, any American
citizen or applicant for citizenship could acquire 160 acres of
public land by residing upon and cultivating it for five years,
and no homesteaded acreage could be seized for debts con-
tracted before acquisition of the land. With these provisions,
the proponents of the bill hoped to ease poverty and limit social and economic conflict in the East.

By 1890, Howells felt that this philosophy had been discarded.
Much of the better public land—land that might be used to give
new opportunities to those in need—had been deeded away to
railroad companies and holding groups, who were interested only
in selling the land for profit.[38] He believed that the congresses
and state legislatures which by 1891 had given away 129,000,000
acres [39] had made a grievous error and that the results of their
work were now showing up in the decreased public domain and
an increased lower class. He apparently did not realize, as many
did not, that most of the land remaining in the public domain
in the 1880's was arid and nonarable and that many Eastern
laborers had neither the money nor the skill to become successful farmers on marginal or submarginal land, even if they had
wished to. By 1894, he saw that the good land was gone,[40] but
even then he was inclined to overvalue the public domain of the
'80's as a place where "the poor might have provided for themselves." [41] With his love of rural life he noted the great intensi-
fication of urban living and placed part of the blame on a corrupt and shortsighted land policy. His position in the 1890's was

to preserve what was left of the public domain and to help struggling farmers throughout the country in every possible way.

One answer to the farm problem was government aid. Howells' own Midwestern background and his friendship with men like Hamlin Garland and J. J. Piatt made him aware of the continuing drop in farm prices during the 1880's and '90's. As a result, he backed Senator Leland Stanford's bill of 1890 proposing to establish government low-interest loans to farmers for mortgage payments.[42] Through such loans Howells believed that farmers could escape the tremendous burden of periodic high-interest payments which ran "ten, twenty and thirty per cent," [43] and thus save money for farm improvement. The scheme, essentially one of substituting government loans for private loans, was one example of how the State could act in the public interest. By aiding the farmer and by discouraging greedy money-lending, it could help stabilize the economy and reward honest work.

Another answer to the farm problem was a direct subsidy to the farmer. Here Howells stepped cautiously, but he apparently felt that the financial uneasiness of 1892-3 demanded some action. A letter of his which appeared in the Boston *Transcript* of January 7, 1893, and was partly reprinted in *Critic* magazine of January 14, 1893, called for aid to the farmer. The events which prompted Howells' action concerned New Hampshire's efforts to conserve its forest lands. These were slowly being depleted by farmers who were cutting down and selling their timber to compensate for poor crops. As depletion continued, state authorities became concerned about the effect on watersheds and natural resources. A commission was appointed to study the problem and considerable discussion resulted as to the proper action of the State in this sphere. Howells, interested in conservation, wrote to the secretary of the commission, J. B. Harrison, his old friend and a contributor to the *Atlantic,* and the letter found its way to the Boston newspaper. Howells wrote:

> You and I love trees perhaps more than dollars, but if we were hill-country farmers and saw that a bit of woodland would help us to pay our taxes and live a little longer in the old house, we would sell the trees and rejoice in the dollars. Let the dollars

come from the State, and your people will keep both the trees and the dollars.[44]

Under Howells' plan, the State would buy the timber and put restrictions on its being cut. By such aid both the farmers and the State would gain. The farmers would have their money, and the State would have its forests. The people of New Hampshire would keep their valuable resources by acting as a community where the community was vitally affected.

Implicit in Howells' reasoning is the idea of molding the human environment. He argues much as John Wesley Powell had argued earlier regarding the semiarid West. When a problem concerns the welfare of all and cannot be satisfactorily settled by individual action, the State should step in and regulate for the benefit of the majority. If man is not to be a blind creature of nature, he must take some part in shaping his universe, whether it be by keeping valuable watersheds in New Hampshire or controlling water rights in Colorado. As did Powell, Howells often saw the individual acting not privately but through the State.

This concept occurs again in Howells' notion of public employment for those who have lost their jobs through technological improvement. He mentions this idea twice in A Traveler from Altruria,[45] and suggests that some provision be made for older people under a similar system.[46] These ideas spring from his belief that any person willing to work should be given work that allows him provision and rest. As Basil March says in A Hazard of New Fortunes, "Nothing less ideal than this satisfies the reason." [47] The natural employer, of course, is the State. When a man is out of work, either temporarily or for a considerable time, he should be able to turn to the State for a job.

What kind of job should the State provide for such an emergency? Works that will be in the public interest, Howells answers. Mr. Homos tell how the Altrurians cared for the industrially unemployed:

We had a continent to refine and beautify; we had climates to change and seasons to modify; a whole system of meteorology to readjust, and the public works gave employment to the multitudes emancipated from the soul-destroying service of shame. I can scarcely give you a notion of the vastness of the improvements undertaken and carried through. . . .[48]

Here in 1893 are the embryonic ideas that were later to blossom forth in the New Deal's Works Progress Administration and the Civilian Conservation Corps. In the novel Howells credits the principle of public works to William Morris, and it is undoubtedly from the English writer that he derived his own thought.* But this should not dim Howells' importance as a transmitter. He was one of the first important American proponents of the concept, and he brought it to the attention of thousands of Americans who had never heard of the creator of News from Nowhere. Moreover, he made the doctrine more respectable than it had even been previously. Before Howells, only those men whom the public generally regarded as "crackpots" espoused such a frankly inflationary scheme, and just two years after Howells endorsed the idea, General Jacob S. Coxey, Greenbacker and Populist and a man widely regarded as a hopeless radical, organized his famous march on Washington to present his public works scheme to President Cleveland. The General was arrested for walking on the White House lawn and the nation enjoyed a good laugh. But for the dean of American letters to include public works in his Utopian economics was a different story, and Howells' remarks undoubtedly had some effect both on the American public and on American reformers. In 1900, the plan of public employment became an official plank in the Socialist Party platform, and it was to remain there until 1932 when President Hoover organized the first Public Works Administration, an agency that President Roosevelt was later to expand during the depression of that decade. Almost forty years after Howells talked of public works to aid the unem-

---

* Howells, A Traveler from Altruria, page 277. The idea, of course, also has American antecedents, though probably not a great number. John Hicks simply says the principle was "not entirely unknown" previous to 1890 (The American Nation, 184). One of the first demands for public employment on record occurred in New York City in 1808 when a band of unemployed sailors clamored for work on the roads of the city. Probably similar calls were heard throughout the nineteenth century during depression times, though many of them never reached print.

ployed and "refine and beautify" a continent, the United States
government instituted a program very similar to that of the
Altrurians.

Greater governmental action—this is the principle behind almost every one of Howells' specific suggestions for reform. Only
through such action can there be a preservation of the public
domain, state subsidies to farmers, provision for older citizens,
and employment for the technologically displaced. But this type
of reform, Howells is careful to point out, should not be tied
to particular measures. It should express a general philosophy
of government. Intervention, he says in effect, is justifiable when
the public interest obviously demands it. During the streetcar
strike in *A Hazard of New Fortunes,* Basil March asks if the
public is not so concerned that the city should step in:

> What amuses me is to find that in an affair of this kind the
> roads have rights and the strikers have rights, but the public
> has no rights at all. The roads and the strikers are allowed to
> fight out a private war in our midst—as thoroughly and pre-
> cisely a private war as any we despise the Middle Ages for hav-
> ing tolerated—as any street war in Florence or Verona—and to
> fight it out at our pains and expense, and we stand by like sheep,
> and wait till we get tired. . . . We have no hold upon the
> strikers; and we're so used to being snubbed and disobliged by
> common carriers that we have forgotten our hold on the roads,
> and always allow them to manage their own affairs in their own
> way, quite as if we had nothing to do with them, and they
> owed us no services in return for their privileges.[49]

Howells then makes his own recommendation in the words
of Colonel Woodburn. Since the strikers had accepted and the
owners had refused state arbitration, the colonel remarks that

> . . . if he was boss of this town he would seize the roads on
> behalf of the people, and man 'em with policemen, and run 'em
> till the managers had come to terms with the strikers.*

---

* Howells, *A Hazard of New Fortunes,* II, 214. Howells was more
than once disturbed by management's refusal to arbitrate. In his "Was
There Nothing to Arbitrate?" *Harper's Weekly,* XXXII (April 21, 1888),
286, he takes strong issue with the Chicago, Burlington and Quincy Rail-

Government then had an obligation to press actively for public welfare. It should protect its citizenry from a private war which kept men and women away from parts of the city and children away from school.[50] It could, and should, intervene when the battles of management and labor threaten the entire population. That the public was affected in some strikes as greatly as the employer or striker was obvious. For Howells, Jefferson's dictum, "The government that governs the least, governs the best," was obsolete, and later he was to poke fun at the idea.[51]

Howells had other suggestions too. Why shouldn't the State take over public ownership of mountain and forest areas and maintain national parks, he asked in 1895.[52] Though the National Park Act was not passed until 1916, actual creation of federal parks began with Yellowstone in 1872, and Howells joined his voice with those asking for more reserves. Under Howells' plan, the State would support summer hotels at nominal rates and offer the average man the opportunity for an inexpensive vacation and a short breathing spell from city living. With wages what they were in 1895, the average worker had little chance of getting away to the mountains or lake shores, but Howells predicted that State control and the establishment of reasonable rates would furnish the American family with a new kind of summer living—one that would send it back to the city physically and mentally refreshed. Howells knew that such hopes were far in the future, but he felt that it was important to talk about them.

Another idea that Howells mentioned briefly was that of public control of housing. How such control would be exercised he never specified, but after a walk through the slums on New York's Lower East Side, he was ready to recommend some change from the system of private landlordship.[53] The crowding of three and four families into quarters hardly large enough for one, the lack of adequate sanitation, broken windows, terrible odors, the absence of light or heating, and rents as high as peo-

---

road for shutting the door on negotiations with the Brotherhood of Engineers after the union had agreed to discussion of a wage dispute. Howells comments that both the railroads and unions should remember their public obligations. He says that if the roads refuse to recognize such duties, the government may have to take them over.

ple would pay—all convinced Howells of the need for drastic change. He wrote at the end of his "East Side Ramble" in 1896:

> Upon the present terms of leaving the poor to be housed by private landlords, whose interest it is to get the greatest return of money for the money invested, the very poorest must always be housed as they are now. Nothing but public control in some form or another can secure them a shelter fit for human beings.[54]

With such suggestions, Howells the theoretical socialist gave way to Howells the practical realist. Many of his proposals were attempts at workable reform to remedy an increasingly serious situation. If one accepts Eric Goldman's distinction between a liberal and a socialist (with the reservation, of course, that there is much overlapping) as the difference between a man working within a capitalistic framework to make that framework more flexible and more practical and a man working to establish an entirely new framework in which the State controls all means of production and distribution, William Dean Howells was both a liberal and a socialist.[55] But his great contributions to reform lie in his *liberal* proposals. Probably he saw many of his ideas as eventually working toward a socialistic state, but he did not overlook the fact that others helped adjust the present capitalistic society. They aided conditions as they then existed, and such aid was Howells' immediate interest. It is clear that Howells the socialist, who envisioned a State where all conditions of competitive capitalism have been erased, has had little influence on American society. But as the liberal advocating government intervention in strikes, aid to farmers, and public works for the unemployed, he has been an integral part of an influential force in American culture. On the whole his patchwork has proven much more effective than his new fabric.

But three all-important facts need emphasis here. First of all, Howells was a gadfly in that he constantly moved from one reform to another, often without exploring any question fully. He would comment on such problems as conservation or subsidies to farmers in an essay or novel and then completely neglect them in subsequent writings. From public works, he might go to trust-busting, to public housing, to aid for farmers. He wrote as ideas occurred to him and was a commentator on contemporary events rather than a systematic reformer. Undoubtedly one of the reasons for his literary roving lay in the fact that he was a magazine columnist most of his life and he undoubtedly thought it necessary to make his articles varied and topical. But a more basic reason lies in Howells' philosophy. He was the inheritor of an eighteenth-century humanism which put great stress on being a well-rounded man, and he exemplified this tradition until he died. He consciously varied both his reading and his writing and actively strove for a kind of urbane liberalism which was the antithesis of specialization. For this reason he was more interested in the multiple facets of a large "reform" philosophy than he was in any single reform, and thus his writings often pay the penalty of being diversified and disjointed.

This does not mean, however, that Howells lacked influence with his contemporaries. From his position as a prominent social observer and a leader of American letters, Howells always commanded attention, and many of his readers were far more interested in current events than they were in any system of reform. They read and absorbed his social counsel for over thirty years, and, as we shall see later, for many his words had considerable effect.

A second fact that should be pointed up is Howells' humanitarianism. It is important to emphasize that his socialism began and was sustained because of his concern for human welfare. He regarded socialism as the system most likely to establish good relations among men and give each individual an opportunity for the basic essentials in life. Because he did so, Howells usually looked first at the human factor involved in any proposal of reform. His attitude is evident in his reaction to the notion that times must get worse before getting better, an idea often voiced during the '80's and '90's, and one particularly repugnant to Howells. Conditions were bad enough without wishing them worse, he believed, and if people could not now see faults in the present system, they probably never would. In Altruria, socialism materializes not when times get worse but when the abuse of power becomes too flagrant and the ballot is utilized.[56]

In *The World of Chance,* Howells is even more explicit. Here

one of Hughes' friends expresses the hope that low-tariff supporters will gain control of Congress and cut off import duties,
an action which would result in lower wages for the workers
and eventually a depression. Then, he remarks, there might be
some concerted effort for improvement. Yes, replies Hughes,
"but such hopes as that would make me hate the cause, if anything could. Evil that good may come? Never! Always a good,
and good for evil, that the good may come more and more." [57]
Profoundly humanitarian, Howells could not bear to think that
reform could come only through more misery and poverty. There
was enough of that already. What man needed now was a Christian approach to the problem. "After all, we are our brother's
keepers," he wrote. "We are put into one another's custody in
this world. In the history of the race, that is the most obvious
lesson." [58] For Howells, every man had obvious obligations to
his fellows and should never be indifferent to their wants, not
even when callousness might produce a worthy result.

A third fact is that Howells combined his reform theories with
the American democratic tradition. Even in his most socialistic
proposals, he always advocated using the vote rather than violence to establish change. "The way to have the golden age is
to elect it," [59] old Hughes cries in *The World of Chance,* and
these words reflect Howells' own feelings. He was convinced a
socialist state would result if people remained steadfast and
voted as their consciences dictated. Socialism would and could
come through democracy. In fact, it was absolutely essential
that it do so. Hughes says, "We must have the true America in
the true American way, by reasons, by votes, by laws, and not
otherwise." [60] These are not the words of a Marxist. A socialism
brought about by revolution and class violence was completely
antithetical to everything Howells held dear. The new economic
system could come about only through the old political system.
Howells was adamant on this.

Moreover, in establishing the new state, Howells was willing to
go slowly. His counsel was principally one of patience and evolution. He avoided the immediate expectations of such a man
as Henry George and allowed for a slow and orderly development, a gradual creation of the new society. It is again the socialist Hughes who expresses Howells' thinking when he remarks

that "Our cause has a sacred claim upon all generous and enlightened spirits; they are recreant if they neglect it. But we must be patient, even with indifference; it is hard to bear, but we cannot right it, and we must bear it . . . we must have patience." [61]

Howells made it clear, and Mrs. Homos so indicates in her correspondence, that Altruria was not built in a day.[62] He saw plainly that man must live in the world and therefore must accept its competitive conditions, at least for the present. But improvement could come if man continued to press for it. Hughes says, "When you are in the midst of a battle, as we all are here, you must fight, and fight for yourself, always, of course, keeping your will fixed on the establishment of a lasting peace." [63] In 1888, Howells complimented Edward Everett Hale on his work for reform. You teach patience, he told the Boston clergyman, "with conditions that I believe wrong, but that must be borne, with all the possible alleviations, till they can be very gradually changed." [64]

In this manner Howells recommends both action and patience. It is necessary that man take some immediate measures to lessen poverty and suffering; he must also strive actively for a socialistic state in the future, being prepared for setbacks and slow improvement. The vote and gradual change—these are the instruments for betterment.

In so speaking for democracy and evolution and in forwarding ideas that involved government aid rather than rigid state control, Howells undoubtedly helped the cause of reform. The linking of change with democracy and the formulation of an American version of what many people regarded as a dangerous foreign philosophy attracted readers who saw their own discontent and vague notions about reform crystallized in Howells' books and essays. Much like the Populists, the novelist appealed to the harassed middle and lower classes which were hardest hit by adverse times and periodic depressions. Part of his appeal lay in the fact that Howells himself was a member of the middle class, and the interest, the sincerity of his proposals, as well as his literary position, won him considerable attention. The greatest part of his appeal, however, was probably his belief that cooperation among men was an American tradition and that government enterprise, the direction from which most people expected help, had a long standing in the United States. Howells never looked on socialism as a foreign philosophy; in fact he insisted on its Americanism. After all, he asks in *Stories of Ohio* (1897), weren't all the canals in Ohio built by the State and didn't the sixteen million dollars that they cost come back to the people in the form of new towns, new businesses, new profits? [65] Didn't the United States government build and regulate the National Road in the best interests of all? Weren't there public schools and public dams? [66] The answers were obvious, and they gave hope to people who felt urgently the need for some reform. If the state previously acted in the public interest, why couldn't it act for the same reason now?

This question was perhaps the one most constantly asked in the early 1890's, years filled with hardship and despair. The bank panic of 1893 and the serious depression that followed, the Homestead Strike, the Pullman Strike, the continuing decline of farm prices, the growing protest against big business, all contributed to widespread unrest. The clamor for reform mounted during these years—middle-class businessmen demanded relief from the trusts, miners with silver interests called for a disavowal of the gold standard, farmers heeded Mary Ellen Lease's advice to raise less corn and more hell and insisted on action on commodity prices and railroad rates. The movement was climaxed in 1896 when both the Populists and the Democrats nominated William Jennings Bryan on a platform of major reform.

Howells was swept up in the general excitement, and four of his most important articles were published in the two years preceding the election of 1896—"Are We a Plutocracy?" "Equality as the Basis of Good Society," "The Nature of Liberty," and "Who Are Our Brethren?" These articles underscore the need for change. His political position during the campaign reveals a personal dilemma. He had already called for the adoption of several planks in the platforms of the Populists and Democrats—lower tariffs, government control of natural monopolies, effective action against the trusts—but he disliked the extremist element behind Bryan and the tremendous emphasis put on the adoption of free silver, a plan that he had always opposed.[67] He was a man caught in a buzz saw, and in July he wrote to a friend that he did not know how he would vote.[68]

After Bryan's decisive defeat, the excitement subsided, not because of discouragement, but because of relief. It is one of the ironies of American history that the McKinley Administration, committed to hard money and tight credit, found itself in the midst of an economic boom after 1896. Beginning in the next year, there was a succession of good harvests in America matched by poor ones in Europe, and for the first time since the Civil War, the farmer began to receive higher prices for his crops. In 1898 the military expenditures of the Spanish-American War helped the economy, and in the same year a revolutionary new process of refining gold combined with the discovery of new ore in South Africa and the Klondike to ease the scarcity of hard money. Financial pressures slackened on many occupations, and Americans were able to breathe more freely during the last years of the decade—a decade strangely known as the "Gay Nineties."

The return of prosperity obviously undercut many of the reform positions. The election of 1896 marks the end of an era, and some ideas, formerly regarded as vital, were virtually forgotten. The silver issue was never successfully revived, and trust-busting and other reforms had to wait another day. Farmers, businessmen, miners, laborers all found new opportunities at the end of the century, and the American economic system and governmental philosophy were looked upon more kindly at the end of the century.

Howells' position during these years was firm and undeviating. He believed that change was still vitally needed, some reform absolutely essential. Good times might beguile others, but Howells refused to close his eyes to what he felt were weaknesses in American life. The twentieth century found him still a socialist in principle and still fighting for new laws, some involving old problems, some involving issues facing the new age.

HOWELLS AND REFORM:
1896-1920

FOR MANY YEARS critics have tended to see in Howells' social reform a pattern much like that of a relief map of the eastern United States—a level, undisturbed plain that rises into foothills and mountains in the Alleghenies and then subsides into the flat, placid lands of Ohio and Indiana. The years between 1888 and 1896 are the Alleghenies, high, broad, challenging; the years following are the plains of Howells' native Midwest which stretch westward until they end in the prairies of Kansas and Nebraska. The impression is that Howells the social critic ceased long before Howells the writer. Van Wyck Brooks comments that Howells' interest in reform died after 1896 when the agrarian reform movement died [1] and William Eckstrom remarks that the novelist's social criticism waned in the later '90's before exhausting itself in a final flurry of anti-imperialism.[2]

If one considers only Howells' novels after 1896, he can support this view. Certainly none of the later stories match for social emphasis and significance the Altrurian romances and *The*

World of Chance. But when one considers Howells' total writing, such a position becomes untenable. Howells' articles of the later period clearly reveal that his interest in reform is not dead. Ideas, old and new, crowd his pages, and some of his most provocative statements come after the turn of the century. In fact, in considering Howells' social and economic thinking after 1896, one is first of all struck by its pervasive character. Comments on capitalism, socialism, Christian ethics, prison reform, women's suffrage, and American culture are everywhere in Howells' nonfiction, even in articles on spelling changes and motion pictures.[3] In truth, *this* was Howells' social period. Rather than waning, his interest in reform was intensified during the muckraker era and in the days just before, during, and after the first World War. Moreover, after 1900 Howells was in a perfect position to continue his role as a gadfly of reform because in December of that year he took over the "Editor's Easy Chair" column in *Harper's Monthly,* a position which he held until his death in 1920 and one which allowed him a free range of editorial comment. Undoubtedly the fact that he had to write 3,000 words each month for the magazine provided a stimulus to his thought, but it is clear that this thought continued primarily in a social direction. Tolstoy's books, he said, were disturbers of men's consciences, and Howells continued to hold the same hopes for his own writing.

After McKinley's election and the signs of returning prosperity, one might expect to find Howells more optimistic about the future. As we have seen, he was not. He remained pessimistic because he could see no fundamental change in the order of things. He remembered his own admonition when commenting on Harrison's *Certain Dangerous Tendencies in American Life:*

> . . . very possibly he [the author] might insist that this [prosperity] was a transitory and illusory experience; and that the supine acquiescence of those who confide in it was material for a still more discouraging paper than any he had yet written.[4]

Because he felt this way, Howells voiced serious skepticism when John Jay Chapman's book *Causes and Consequences* offered hope for a better political future because of the decline of the "boss" and the fact that the great fortunes had been made. Though much of the book appealed to him in its criticism of the economic order, Howells found that he was "most pessimistic where he [Chapman] is most optimistic." [5] For Howells, the American culture was still as commercial and competitive as it ever had been, and as long as the businessman, the source of political corruption, remained the social ideal, the situation would not improve:

> There was a time when the business man did not control public affairs, and there came a time with the making of the great fortunes, when he began to do so. This was the time when the boss came into the political world. He came for "what there was in it," and he was and is simply the business man's creature; without the money of the business man the boss could not exist a year, a month . . . I doubt if they [the bosses] have yet been driven finally out, or are in any danger of it; and I do not see how, if we are politically corrupt through our lust of money-getting, we are to purge and live cleanly in conditions which are still as commercial as they were while the great fortunes were making.[6]

In 1898 came another event which kept Howells from being hopeful about the future—the Spanish-American War. All wars were horrible to Howells, but an American adventure in Cuba was particularly abhorrent. In addition to killing American and Cuban and Spanish boys, a terrible thing in itself, it helped consolidate American capitalism. He wrote to his sister Aurelia on April 3, three weeks before the war began:

> I hope you will not be surprised to hear that I think we are wickedly wrong. We have no right to interfere in Cuba, and we have no cause of quarrel with Spain. At the very best we propose to do evil that good may come. If we have war it will be at the cost of a thousand times more suffering than Spain has inflicted or could inflict on Cuba. After war will come the piling up of big fortunes again; the craze for wealth will fill all brains, and every good cause will be set back. We shall have an era of blood-bought prosperity, and the chains of capitalism will be welded on the nation more firmly than ever.[7]

Two weeks later he wrote Henry James in much the same vein, calling the war "stupid and causeless" and adding that "the strange thing about the argument with Spain is that nobody, except the newspapers and politicians, wants war." He was still hopeful, however, that "there is a chance for reason." [8]

On April 20, Congress doomed Howells' hopes and voted into effect President McKinley's declaration of war. During the next two months Howells, along with the rest of the nation, watched the reports coming from Cuba. He seems to have had no fears of an American imperialistic design,[9] possibly because of the Teller Resolution, which was adopted with the declaration of war and stated that the United States had no "intention to exercise sovereignty, jurisdiction, or control over said Island [Cuba] except for pacification thereof" and asserted "its determination, when that is accomplished, to leave the government and control of the Island to its people." [10]

But by the end of July, his views had changed. He was astonished by and contemptuous of the demand made by American politicians for the cession of Puerto Rico and an island in the Ladrones in lieu of Spanish indemnity payments. He wrote Henry James, "Our war for humanity has unmasked itself as a war for coaling stations, and we are going to keep our booty to punish Spain for putting us to the trouble of using violence in robbing her." [11]

Howells' first article on the war, "Our Spanish Prisoners at Portsmouth," appeared in November 1898. Though not primarily anti-imperialistic, it was strongly antiwar. It emphasized the common humanity of all men and the considerate behavior of both the American guards and the Spanish prisoners. Howells asked for greater understanding among men so that "to butcher and capture a lot of wretched Spanish peasants and fishermen, hapless conscripts to whom personally and nationally we were so many men in the moon" [12] will never again be necessary. War to him was "homicide in which there is not even the saving grace of hate, or the excuse of hot blood." [13]

This was Howells' last important mention of the Spanish-American War and its consequences until after the turn of the century when the disposition of the Philippines again brought up the question of imperialism. Though in 1900 the American people had shown their approval of McKinley's conduct of the war by re-electing him after a campaign waged mainly on the issue of imperialism, American colonialism remained largely un-implemented until 1901, when, after the defeat of the Philippine native insurrection, the American civil government was first established in Manila. This action caused a final flurry of anti-imperialistic writing in the first two years of the new century, and Howells soon found himself in the midst of it.

The brief comment that the Filipino patriot, Jose Rizal, was killed by the Spaniards "a few years before we bought a con-trolling interest in their crimes against his country" [14] began Howells' anti-imperialistic remarks in April 1901. A month later he briefly mentioned the Spanish-American War "whose Dead Sea fruit is still turning to ashes on our lips." [15] These short notes, both made in the "Editor's Easy Chair," were but prel-udes to the quiet but scathing indictment which appeared in June in the *North American Review*. Here Howells remarked that the war had concluded two centuries of American moral supremacy. An era had ended. The war implied, he wrote,

> the close of the peculiar mission of America to mankind. We shall probably be richer and we shall be stronger even than we are now, but the American shall hardly again be the son of the morn-ing, toward which the struggling people turned their eyes with the hope at least of sympathy . . . . once in our national conscious-ness, at least, to the mystification of the unbelieving and im-penitent world outside, we stood for something different from anything a people ever stood for before. Call it universal liberty or instinctive justice, or even by the tedious name of humanity, it was something novel and brave and generous, and it differ-enced us from all the monarchies limited and unlimited, the conquerors, the oppressors.[16]

In this article Howells reveals his love of that earlier America, its democracy, its fundamental belief in man and his ability to find the good. He saw the imperialistic adventure as a reversal of these ideals. Now America, the home of a belief in self-de-termination, had decided that some men could not find the good without its help. Moreover, Congress had decreed in effect that the Constitution did not follow the Flag and that the Filipinos, though under United States jurisdiction, did not have the rights of American citizens. In January 1902 Howells spoke out again:

> We are conquerors like the rest; we have an imperial empire, with a Constitution that does not cover that empire, but leaves out in the cold a great many Americans, who seem to be trying to warm themselves in their place by making it hot for us in ours. They [older observers of the American scene] could only hearken to the call of duty as it was in those who conceived of men as best left to work out their own destinies, while the new conception of duty is that other men can better work out their destinies for them.[17]

The Filipinos, he concluded, had a right to believe in the Declaration of Independence.[18]

Like his friend Mark Twain, Howells opposed imperialism on the grounds of humanity. For him the goal of universal brotherhood was constantly a higher one than that of material gain or colonial power, and imperialism was a barrier to such a goal. Democracy in literature, he wrote in *Criticism and Fiction* (1891), seeks to tell men they are more alike than unlike, to help them know one another better and see their fraternity.[19] And, as Howells emphasized, this fraternity extended beyond national boundaries. Thus in May 1902, he reacted strongly against the suggestion found in the will of Cecil Rhodes that England attempt eventually to establish an Anglo-Saxon empire over the entire world. Such "race-patriotism" was simply another name for imperialism to Howells. He opposed it, he said, in the ideal of humanity, the ideal

> that the various races of man shall work out their own destiny in their own way, without our very fallible guidance or control . . . the great Dr. Johnson once declared that patriotism was the last refuge of scoundrels. It is not easy to go beyond this, but it is a pity that so apt a notion could not be carried a little farther with respect to the race-patriotism which some people are just now trying to substitute for the old-fashioned notion of humanity, once the ideal of high-thoughted men.[20]

Howells' anti-imperialistic remarks continued through most of 1902. In July he wrote that the Spanish-American War had "tempted us into a lust of dominion which we have gratified by cruelties unimaginable of Americans before." [21] In December his ironic poem, "The Christmas Spirit," asks Santa Claus to

> Look well about you, see what has been done:
> How life smiles everywhere beneath the sun;
> See the whole world at peace, from the Transvaal
> To the far Philippines, one rapture all
> Of peace with freedom.[22]

Even in the years following 1903, when the issue was largely forgotten, Howells was not completely silent. In 1904 and 1905, he again commented on imperialism,[23] and in 1913 he showed he still remembered the war. He wrote that to give a Spanish boy a scholarship to an American school "was a greater thing than to have taken Cuba from Spain and bought the Philippines when we had seized them already and led the Filipinos to believe that we meant to give their island to them." [24] Even in 1916 Howells stirred against imperialism and criticized Wilson for his "Mexican muddling" in Vera Cruz.[25]

All in all, Howells was, to use the words of Samuel Johnson, a good hater. Moreover he shared with the venerable doctor an eighteenth-century cosmopolitanism which caused him to question narrow patriotism and the idea of "the white man's burden." Howells' wide travels and his own democratic beliefs left him with the conviction that all men had the ability to rule themselves. It seemed apparent to him that for one country to attempt to control another was morally wrong and no amount of squirming or rationalizing could make it right. He believed all men had the right to decide their own destinies, and nothing shook this belief.

II

When Howells turned to seek the reasons for imperialism, he ran directly into capitalism and the concept of Social Darwinism. The latter idea grew out of Darwin's theory of evolution and became the doctrine of the survival of the fittest in the

social and business as well as the natural world. It found favor
in some circles of acquisitive capitalism and often provided the
rationale for a dog-eat-dog competition through which the most
unprincipled rose to the top. Andrew Carnegie's statement that
economic competition, though hard on the individual, was "best
for the race, because it insures the survival of the fittest in every
department" [26] and John D. Rockefeller's comment that "the
American Beauty rose can be produced in all the splendor and
fragrance which bring cheer to its beholder only by sacrificing
the early buds which grow up around it" [27] exemplified a definite
attitude at the turn of the century. To such men, imperialism
was a kind of individualism and simply the way of progress, the
means by which the stronger triumphed over the weaker and
perpetuated advanced thought and technology.

Howells, as we have seen, took a humanistic view. He seems
to have accepted Darwinian thought on the natural level, but
he could never assent to its application to the social world. In
June 1902, speaking of England's attempt "to sweep the Boers
from the Veldt," he wrote:

> The brutalization of the civilized world, within the last three
> or four decades, undoubtedly began with the misinterpretation of
> evolution, when the strongest read itself into the survival of the
> fittest. This gross delusion took practical form in the armament
> of the nations, and . . . the feeling that the great power, when
> it chose, could stamp out the life of any little people.[28]

Two years later he spoke out more fully. He commented that
the nineteenth century, in allying man with the brute and for-
mulating the doctrine that might was right, bereft men of the
humanity which the ages had evolved as an ideal of conduct.[29]
He compared the eighteenth and the nineteenth centuries—the
eighteenth which if it "could have lasted a few years longer . . .
might have ended in a golden age" and the nineteenth whose
"tale of wars and woes . . . almost eclipses its achievements in
literature, science, and finance."

> The one tended to unite, to fraternize, and to civilize man-
> kind, and the other tended to divide, to provincialize, and to

brutalize mankind. Under the specious show of struggles for na-
tionality, for the unification of races, at one time, and at a later
time in the guise of conquests for the exploitation of the weaker
people by the stronger in every part of the world, especially in
the free and enlightened part, the nineteenth century was false
to the example of the eighteenth, in which the greatest thoughts
and deeds were for freedom.[30]

In 1907, after Japan had defeated Russia and absorbed Korea,
Howells took note of the situation by commenting that the
righteous plea of a need for expansion was merely the "modern
name for conquest" and a screen by which the strong overcame
the weak.[31]

Thus for Howells, imperialism and Social Darwinism were
twin evils which, singly or linked, had no place in a society which
professed to honor the dignity and worth of the individual. Both
concepts had only one justification, strength, and the ideals which
meant the most to Howells—morality, humanity, democracy—
had little influence in a system where might was right.

III

One of the most significant of the proposals that Howells publicly supported before the turn of the century was the principle
of arbitration as a means of settling international disputes. In
1896 he endorsed negotiation as the proper method to adjudicate
the quarrel between England and Venezuela over the boundary
between the latter country and British Guiana. This position al-
lied Howells with those who were advocating arbitration before
the idea became popular with the peace leagues that grew out
of the Spanish-American War. As a small nation militarily, the
United States had always favored international arbitration, but
it was not until the latter part of the 1890's that there was great
popular support for the idea. Then partly in reaction to American
imperialism and partly because of the growing wave of humanitarianism, various groups began campaigning for peaceful mediation between nations. Part of the impetus for this movement
came in 1897 when official negotiations were begun on the question of the boundary between Venezuela and British Guiana.
When this question first arose in 1895 and threatened to erupt

into war, President Cleveland, acting under a broad interpretation of the Monroe Doctrine, demanded that England and Venezuela arbitrate their claims and set up an American commission
to consider such claims.

Howells disagreed with Cleveland's policy of compulsory
arbitration because he saw it might well lead to war if England
refused to arbitrate. He proposed instead a plan of voluntary
arbitration by which the United States would agree to act as
intermediary between the disputants if they wished to submit
their titles for settlement. This plan would allow America to
serve justice and at the same time bow out with dignity if England declined to negotiate. He wrote:

> We might have still been proud of proposing arbitration to
> England . . . and we might have retired with unimpaired dignity
> from the refusal she had clearly the right to make us. That prin-
> ciple of arbitration, which we invented, is much more honorable
> to us, and much worthier our patriotic emotion, than any war
> we could wage in an attempt to make it compulsory.[32]

Fortunately both England and Venezuela accepted the American commission's invitation to present their cases and then later,
in February of 1897, officially agreed to abide by the decision of
a newly chosen board of settlement. This action promoted international negotiation, and after 1899, when the first Hague
conference took place, the United States committed itself to a
policy of voluntary negotiation before the Hague Permanent
Court of Arbitration. Later that same year America and Mexico
took the first case before the Hague Tribunal when they sub-
mitted the Pious Fund controversy.

Howells supported the position of arbitration during the succeeding years. In 1907 he voiced the hope for complete international negotiation of all differences through the Hague Court.

> Providence may not choose to punish our sins in the old way,
> that is, through war and destruction but may favor our redemp-
> tion by means of arbitration. . . . Let us hope that this is so,
> for in the old way there was a great deal of injustice incidentally
> done, and myriads of innocent people suffered, before the real

offenders were reached and punished, or sometimes not punished
or even reached.[33]

He referred to "that future Hague Conference, from which we
are hoping so much." [34]

During these years the United States implemented its policy
of arbitration by a series of bilateral treaties with European and
South American nations. Between 1908 and 1910 the Senate approved no less than twenty-two arbitration pacts which provided
for negotiation of all matters of legal or interpretive nature for
a five-year period. These pacts were only steps in the direction
of total negotiation since they provided no safeguard against
military aggression or any contingency not covered by treaty,
but in 1910 it appeared that they might provide the foundation
for future agreements which would make arbitration mandatory
on a wider level.

Obviously pleased with such progress and with the prospects
for arbitration in general, Howells was enthusiastic in August
1911. He believed there was a real chance that the "experiment
in international arbitration" might bring world peace. He wrote,
"During the spring and summer . . . there have been hopes of
peace on earth, such as could not have been reasonably cherished
at any other time since the heavenly hosts were heard praising
God and prophesying good will to men." [35] Though by August,
as Howells pointed out, some of the bloom had faded from the
rose because of heavy armaments in Europe, he was still encouraged by the fact that America, England, and France had
gone to the arbitration table and by the possibility that Japan,
Austria, Russia, and Germany might go too.[36]

Later, 1914 was to provide a tragic denouement to Howells'
optimism, but from 1896 on, Howells was a constant promoter of
international negotiation. His humanitarianism was, of course,
responsible for his strong feelings. He commented in 1911, "The
lesson of all wars is peace: when will the nations learn it?" [37]
Arbitration became for him the logical substitute for warfare,
and what reasoning men should work for. After 1917, he abandoned this pacifistic position and supported the American war
effort. He viewed the conflict as a struggle between autocracy
and democracy and was horrified at reported German atroci-

ties.[38] But, as Gibson and Arms note, Howells never glorified war as such, as many Americans did,[39] and he undoubtedly believed in the principle of arbitration until the end of his life.

IV

Just before the turn of the century, Howells also made an attack, though a sidelong one, against a specific trust. In February and March 1896, he wrote three articles on the high price of drama tickets and on the need for a government-subsidized theater. His main argument was that the price of two dollars for orchestra seats and a dollar and a half for regular seats was too high and often went for needless stage luxuries or to satisfy the manager's greed. He believed that the theater, a medium of education, should be open to everyone and not just to those who could pay.[40] Moreover, Howells reasoned, by shutting itself off from the middle class and "the wholesome criticism of the best of the American public," the theater was becoming indecent and in need of censorship.[41] He noted that France and Austria had partial government control over theaters and felt that neither subsidy nor regulation was alien to the American spirit, which had established building commissioners to inspect tenements and a board of education to supervise the schooling of the young. The theater, he wrote, should be

> frankly recognized as a factor in popular education, which continues its work life long, and teaches by the strongest appeals to the imagination, and to the unfading interests in human passions, human sorrows, human joys. It is, whatever we may say against it, the great school of morals, of the vital things beside which the knowledges of the textbooks are not important, however important they are in themselves.[42]

Howells offered three alternatives for improvement: the establishment of one public theater in a city, the control of all theaters by the Board of Education, or the authorization of free monthly performances of suitable plays. If any of these plans was adopted, Howells believed the quality of the drama would at once improve. Prices would come down and plays "morally and aesthetically inferior" would not draw.[43]

Howells said no more about the theater until 1898. In the meantime a group of influential producers and theater owners had succeeded in setting up a theatrical trust in New York, Philadelphia, and other large cities. Klaw and Erlanger, the Frohmans, and others had established in 1896 a central booking office through which they controlled both the plays and the actors in theaters throughout the country. Many people in the profession were defiant, but few could afford to buck the syndicate, and by 1898 the group had great power.[44]

Howells' first reaction to the trust was hostile. He wrote:

> Not merely one industry, but civilization itself is concerned [in the theater trust], for the morals and education of the public are directly influenced by the stage. Everyone who takes a pride in the art of his country must regret a monopoly of the theater, for that means "business" and not art.[45]

Then in February 1898, he devoted a column in *Harper's Weekly* to the theatrical trust and the trust principle in general. He mentioned no names, but in his jocular, ironic manner he often hit effectively at the theater syndicate:

> It has indeed driven some great actors who oppose it to making speeches against it, but in the houses which it pre-empts it causes the band to play when they come before the curtain for this purpose and drowns their voices quite as if it were a paternal power dealing with oratory from the scaffold.
>
> The behavior of the trust has of course threatened the prosperity of the theatrical profession. . . . If we had any drama, it would be equally fatal to our drama, but as we have none, our dramatists can safely challenge the trust to do its worst. Upon the same ground our public may defy it, for in the sense of a public with a taste of its own, or any intelligence concerning the theater, we have no more public than drama.[46]

For Howells, the great threat was always that men of talent could be "bought up by the trust and set to work on subjects selected by the directors, who would know much better [than the writers do] what our people want." [47]

This criticism of the theatrical trust marks a new interest for

Howells between 1896 and 1900, but it was closely linked with what had gone before. Included in Howells' remarks on the theater were constant comments on business avarice and the gospel of wealth, two evils that Howells was to attack for the rest of his life. From now on the strictures against the buy-cheap-sell-dear philosophy were going to be made primarily in the magazines, not in the novels, and in such terms as these on the high price of theater seats:

> If they [the wealthy] alone can pay for them, they alone have the right to them. That is the business view, and I always like to take the business view; it flatters my vanity; it makes me feel like a business man. I insist that this is the only test that can be applied in such cases. One might as well say that a poor person ought to have nice things to eat, or handsome clothes to wear, as say he ought to have an evening of artistic pleasure at the theater. Nothing could be more repugnant to the spirit of our institutions, nothing more un-American . . . there is nothing I am clearer about than that no poor person is entitled to a refined pleasure, for the simple and sufficient reason that he cannot pay for it.[48]

V

Howells' censure of the theatrical monopoly is indicative of his social comment after 1896 in that it reveals his continued concern for domestic reform, a concern which matched his interest in imperialism, warfare, and arbitration. In such comment his weapons of attack were again primarily nonfictional, though in *The Landlord at Lion's Head* (1897) Howells does make some pertinent remarks on equality and the middle class.[49] As before, his activities were primarily those of a gadfly. Sometimes his efforts were short articles, sometimes a paragraph, sometimes only a single sentence in an essay devoted to other topics. For example, in discussing the ideal of military duty in "Our Spanish Prisoners at Portsmouth," Howells hopes out loud that "duty will yet become the civic ideal, when the peoples shall have learned to live for the common good, and are united for the operation of the industries as they now are for the hostilities." [50]

Many of Howells' ideas were not new. As one might expect in a muckraking age, he continued to criticize economic in-

dividualism and competition. It is true that his criticism of capitalism and his sponsorship of socialism were more diffused
after 1900, but they never disappeared from his work. He ab-
horred, he wrote, the never-ending struggle for economic gain
that existed under a competitive system.[51] He believed that
capitalism could not bring great prosperity without great ad-
versity, as day could not exist without night.[52] He said that the
United States formerly had chattel slavery; now it had industrial
slavery.[53] He re-emphasized his approval of socialism and reform.
Interest rates he called a "wicked pinch on the debtor," and said
that if a man were willing to work, society should guarantee him
a living wage.[54] He remarked that the best way to distribute
wealth was to give it back to those whose labor had made it.[55]
He reiterated that the ballot box was the proper method of reform and that compromises and part-way measures were necessary because all change could not be accomplished at once.[56]

Still, even with this repetition, Howells' creativeness was surprising. For a man who was fifty-nine in 1896, Howells revealed
a remarkable mental agility during the next twenty-four years.
He continued to produce or popularize new ideas throughout
the period and, though outdone by the exposé writers, he undoubtedly continued to influence a select circle of readers. His
support was sought for various causes, and his writing lent certain reforms a prestige they would not otherwise have had.

The fertility of Howells' thought in the twentieth century
is most evident in his proposals for social reform. Here one of his
favorite topics was the improvement of the American penal
system. This subject had interested Howells in the late '80's and
early '90's when he had taken a strong stand against capital
punishment [57] and written a book to discuss the relative merits
of justice and mercy,[58] but it was not until after the turn of the
century that he made a number of specific suggestions for reform.
In all, between 1903 and 1915, Howells wrote no less than ten
articles which dealt wholly or in part with penal reformation,
and in time he became an influential speaker for a more humane
philosophy.

One of his major proposals was the abolition of the death
sentence. Although in 1866 he had derided the notion of "sen-
timental" justice for killers,[59] Howells later changed his mind

and from 1888 on was a critic of the eye-for-an-eye philosophy. His strongest objections were based on humanitarian or Christian grounds. In 1900 he wrote to the Anti-Death Penalty League of Massachusetts:

> I think capital punishment a legal atrocity, and a species of homicide, incomparably more cruel than most private murders, since it inflicts death after long knowledge of death to come has multiplied its terrors for the victim. It is one of the most useless pieces of wickedness left in the world.[60]

Four years later, Howells repeated his stricture. "We have to face again the fact that on humanitarian grounds State homicide seems more barbarous and abominable than any but the most exceptional private murder, since it adds the anguish of fore-knowledge to the victim's doom." [61] Then Howells continued in irony:

> . . . many disciples of One whose teaching superseded the old law of an eye for an eye, and a life for a life, hold it [capital punishment] little less than of divine ordinance. It is not, then, for a lay brother to question its inspired origin, and I do not question it. I accept it with all its possible aberrations from justice, in the case of those who perish innocently by it, and in the case of the others who merely die a thousand deaths in view of the death they are doomed to.[62]

Howells' second criticism of capital punishment was based on utilitarian grounds. The death penalty did not deter, he said, and thus served no useful purpose. In 1904, in an imaginary conversation with Justice concerning the execution of three brothers who had murdered their uncle, the higher journalist, one of Howells' fictitious disguises, says:

> . . . the benefit to the community has been said to lie in the deterrent consequences of the punishment, but it appears not to deter. There was Czolgocz [the assassinator of McKinley]: but even the swift certainty of his fate did not deter the eldest of those miscreant brothers from boasting that he was going to give his uncle a Czolgocz shot in the stomach. His fate incited to

crime, if anything . . . in countries like Italy and Switzerland, and even that wicked Russia where your extreme penalty is unknown, the life imprisonment is not less deterrent, if it's not more . . . I say that your electric chair like your garrote, your guillotine, your gallows, your block, your leaden mace, is a failure in the very point [deterrence] where its success could alone serve the community.[63]

Throughout succeeding years Howells continued to point out the nondeterrence of the death penalty, and in 1915 he devoted an entire column of the "Editor's Easy Chair" to American penology in general and to deterrent punishment in particular. He complimented Thomas Mott Osbourne, the warden at Ossining, for his emphasis on the rehabilitation of prisoners and remarked that the warden "could invite his friends of established penology to observe that deterrent punishment does not deter . . . the only way to make punishment truly deterrent is to make it anticipative." [64] Later in the same article he wrote:

If they [proponents of capital punishment] had been logical, they might appositively ask themselves where the deterrent force of punishment lay, if within a year after those four men were put to death for a ruthless assassination, quite the same sort of murder was done by the same sort of men. The lives which the state took might almost as well have been spared . . . .[65]

Despite such comments by Howells and other writers, during the first years of the century there was no widespread movement to abolish the death sentence. The subject was widely debated in the magazines of the time, most articles favoring greater leniency, but conservative reaction proved strong and few laws were changed.

Another prison reform that Howells constantly pursued was the proposal to pay inmates during their imprisonment; six articles between 1913 and 1916 make some mention of this plan. Without some kind of payment, Howells reasoned, an inmate was usually worse off financially when he left than when he entered prison and became an "exasperated beggar whom . . . no one will employ and very few befriend." [66] Men like that had nothing before them but more crime. Wives and children were often forced into the streets to work or beg during the husband's imprisonment. Such a system punished the innocent and was the reverse of justice.[67]

Howell's suggestion was that the criminal be paid union wages for his work during imprisonment and that the money be given to his family or, if he had no family, returned to him on his leaving prison. In this way, released men would "have money enough to live on till they could prove themselves worthy of honest work." [68] Howells thought it only just to pay a man for his hire. The state had a right to imprison a criminal, but it had no right to rob him during that imprisonment.[69]

By 1915, many years after Howells had originally conceived the idea and seven after he had specifically pushed it in an article in the *North American Review* ("Some Unpalatable Suggestions"), some results were achieved. In that year a plan to pay wages to prisoners was recommended to the American Prison Association after a successful experiment by the Kansas City penal authority.[70] Later the plan was accepted at the state prison in Ossining, New York, and it gradually won acceptance throughout the country. Today most states have laws which provide for payments to prisoners, though some have dropped the system of wages in favor of an allowance plan.

Other reforms that Howells supported were better prison conditions (present prisons breed criminals, he said); [71] a Court of Rehabilitation, a plan that eventually evolved into part of the Parole Board; [72] speedier justice for the suspect who was often detained in jail "until it is convenient for the State to try him, while all the sagacity of the police and all the ingenuity of the prosecution are employed in extorting and accumulating proofs of his guilt"; [73] and some restitution on the part of the State if a man was proved innocent.[74] This last point was one on which Howells was particularly plain-spoken. A man accused of a crime spent months of time and energy in court, was forced to pay a lawyer to defend him, was cast under suspicion in the eyes of his friends and community, and, if at last proved innocent, was dismissed by his prosecutors without even an apology. Such treatment was obviously unfair, and in Howells' penal Utopia, Barataria, all prisoners are accorded a civic dinner, a public notice of acquittal, and full financial and social reparation after their innocence has been established.[75]

Howells was not original in his proposals. Without exception, all his ideas had been suggested by other men during the nineteenth century, or even earlier.[76] In fact, in taking up problems of prison self-government, honor systems, and reformatories, many criminologists had advanced far beyond Howells' reforms. But Howells was a forerunner in that, along with Orlando Lewis, Thomas Mott Osbourne, and others, he did much to popularize prison reform. This movement gained considerable momentum after 1900 and particularly after 1910, and Howells had a significant part in keeping certain of its objectives before the public.

VI

Another aspect of American life that interested Howells was the question of women's suffrage. His interest in the feminist issue, like his concern for prison reform, antedated 1900, but most of his writing on the subject came in the twentieth century. Here again Howells was a commentator, a promoter of change, a gadfly. His support of the suffrage movement came during a period of great debate on the question, and as a social observer he undoubtedly wanted to record his views.

Most of Howells' comments came at a period of low fortunes for the suffragettes, that is, between 1896 and 1910. During this time not a single state granted full political rights to women, though four states, Wyoming, Colorado, Utah, and Idaho, had done so by 1896. Two important reasons for this failure were the opposition of the liquor interests, who feared women would shut up the saloons and vote for prohibition, and the antagonizing tactics of some of the feminist leaders. Perhaps the real explanation, however, lay in the inertia of the majority of American women. Harold Faulkner in his book *The Quest for Social Justice 1898–1914* remarks that one of the most potent influences holding back feminine suffrage was "the passive indifference of the great majority of . . . women," [77] and Howells recorded this same idea in 1906. "Till women can make up their minds to demand and accept its [the suffrage's] responsibilities, possibly they will do best to let it alone. When they want it, they will have it . . . ." [78]

Howells' main argument in support of equal suffrage was a democratic one. Women's rights, he said, were "merely human rights"; and since women lived and acted within the environment of the State, they should have the right to vote on its practices.[79] Moreover, women were obliged to pay state and federal taxes, and the democratic linkage of taxation and representation would seem to give them "the right to vote which in a republic seems logically to go with the duty to pay." [80]

A second reason for Howells' advocacy was his feeling that women would help American politics, that they would bring a rational element to the democratic process that would strengthen popular government. Women, he commented, "are far better educated, for the most part, than our men, and their tastes, if not their minds, are more cultivated. Our men read the newspapers, but our women read the books." [81]

This rational quality was apparent in women of all classes, Howells thought, but he was particularly interested in "the minds and merits of the women of the masses."

> The women of the lower classes do not drink, they do not even smoke . . . they keep the house and they make the earnings of their husbands and themselves go far in the practical application of political economy . . . almost always they are the betters of their menkind in mind as in heart; and when they get the vote they will naturally come to the help of their brethren of the enlightened classes, as far as these are truly enlightened, and by their accession they will reduce the ignorant and vicious majority.[82]

As Howells suggests here, the moral, as well as the rational, nature of women would have its effect on elections. No longer, he hoped, would the political tone of the country be so crude, the parade of selfish politicians so constant. Women could be a real help to good governement. Like many other men of the Victorian era, Howells seems to have accepted the idea of an innate morality in women, a quality that men did not have. He paraphrased the Spanish writer Palacio Valdés in saying that man was "principally an intellectual being, woman a moral being":

The ideal of goodness, of beauty, of justice never leaves her eyes. Unlike man, even in her deepest degradation, she always believes in her own soul. Perhaps for this reason women forgive themselves more easily for their sins; they know these sins do not touch the purity of their being.[83]

If this moral force could be translated into political effectiveness, Howells felt that corruption and other evils might be given a thorough airing. At the very least, some advances in political efficiency could be made if women were included in the electorate. He never wavered in these ideas. After political equality had finally been won in 1920, Howells remarked that, though some women would still do ridiculous things, he believed that the majority of new voters would sober the country by their good sense and dignity and bring a real competence to managing a world of which men had admittedly made a mess.[84]

VII

During the final twenty years of his life, Howells continued to advance proposals for greater governmental action. He recommended again the advantages of old-age pensions for working men and asked Americans to consider the Australasian plan of subsidies to farmers.[85] He advocated the establishment of state inns, which he felt were no more socialistic than public schools or state roads—inns on which the management "would not be forced to make a profit large enough in two or three months to pay the cost of a year's maintenance." [86] He approved of plans that gave waste acres to the veterans of World War I and offered free instruction in reading and writing.[87] He favored the imposition of the income tax as a means to check the accumulation of great fortunes.[88]

The method of promoting governmental action was, as before, through the ballot box. But Howells was no longer so naive as he had been in the 1880's when he thought that selfishness was the primary reason the working man did not vote in reform. He continued to mention human selfishness,[89] but he now seemed to have recognized more fully the fact that economic power was political power. In 1899, reviewing Thorstein Veblen's *The Theory of the Leisure Class,* Howells wrote:

It is idle to suppose because the leisure class, which with us is the moneyed class, does not hold public office that it does not control public affairs; and possibly it has always controlled them more than we have imagined. The present proof is in the fact that the industrial classes, with all the means of power in their hands, are really powerless in any contest with a group of rich men; it is almost impossible for the people to balk the purpose of such a group; to undo what money has done has been so impossible, with all the apparatus of the elections, the legislatures, the courts, that there is hardly yet an instance of the kind in our history.[90]

Although Howells saw clearly the political power of wealth, his pessimism about defeating the wealthy passed, and three years later he was again recommending the ballot as the proper means of political change.[91] In 1902 he was heartened by the election of a Labor Party candidate to the mayoralty in Hartford, Connecticut. This town had formerly been dominated by wealth, but now "for almost the first time they [the working men] realized that as voters they are the majority, and that the majority can always change any state of things if it does not like it. Acting upon their sense of this fact they have given themselves the luxury of a peaceful triumph." [92]

The democratic process, therefore, was still the method of political change. Under this system Howells was hopeful that socialism would yet come to America. After the turn of the century, he continued to speak for the new economic system, although little jabs replaced the more roundhouse swings of the Altrurian romances, and his remarks, instead of developing into articles or sections in a book, were often short and concise. For example, during his stay in England in 1904, Howells made note of British progress in establishing socialism and reported it to his American readers. Socialism, he said, had passed from "debated principle to accomplished fact." [93] Most progress had been made in municipal control of transportation and public services. He remarked that

socialism has been embodied in so many admirable works that the presumption is rather in favor of it as something truly conservative. It is not, as with us, still under a ban of prejudice too ignorant to know in how many things it is already effective.[94]

In 1909, Howells wrote that England had a state which was "far more the servant of the people in fetching and carrying, in guarding them from hard masters and succoring them in their need, than the republic which professes to derive its just powers from the consent of the governed." [95]

With these little comments on socialism Howells continued to prick the American public during the twentieth century. His belief in the eventual establishment of socialism in America never seems to have faltered until the very last years of his life. Public proprietorhip, he said in 1909, would one day supersede all private ownership.[96] Human nature and socialism would some day be perfected in America.[97] But during the first World War, his views were given a test. At first pleased by the quiet and effective operation of the national economy by governmental boards and administrations formed after America's entry into the war, Howells was moved to write in April 1918:

> The instant realization of State Socialism in our polity is something that would not have less than astounded the nation in any other year, but in our Annus Mirabilis [1917] it has "overcome us like a summer cloud without our special wonder," and without apparent opposition from either labor or capital. It is as if it were as entirely the course of nature that the nation should collectively control and market its fuel and food as that it should produce them. There has been scarcely a murmur from the most capitalistically minded of our journals, and whatever is left of the doctrines of the Manchester school has been . . . silent on the lips of its surviving disciples . . . .[98]

The war with its demand for some over-all authority had given socialism its first real chance in America. For Howells, the dream was on the horizon. "Socialism is an old-fashioned bugaboo now," he wrote in September 1917.[99] It seemed as though the land of the free was actually going to employ state socialism. Or was it? Slowly, almost imperceptibly the dream began to slip away.

By November 1918, Howells was not sure that socialism was going to last. Though the government had now assumed control of the telephones, telegraph, shipyards, and railroads in addition to food and fuel, Howells now saw the strong hostility of many people to such control and was himself vaguely dissatisfied with some aspects of the government program. He intimated that socialism had come through governmental decree and not by popular demand and that such a socialism was based on a shaky foundation. "The accomplished fact," he wrote, "doesn't seem so very accomplished after all." [100]

After the war, amid demands of return to "normalcy" and the wave of antiradicalism which swept the United States after Russian bolshevism became a world power, Howells saw the government boards and administrations dissolved and a popular revulsion against socialism take place. In his last "Editor's Easy Chair" (April 1920), one of the most disheartened columns he ever wrote, he ironically pictures two socialistic Martians visiting the United States and wryly observes their reactions. They are surprised when told that "socialism isn't at all in favor just now" and that a belief in socialism "could keep some of you out of our legislative bodies." [101] The two give a public lecture concerning the civilization on Mars and are amazed to find that socialism is "confounded with all sorts of American incivicism." [102] Their lecture causes a riot, and people begin to wonder if they can be good Americans. Finally the pair are deported to Russia "upon the theory that they are Bolshevists." [103] The American Altruria had collapsed.

Plainly Howells was embittered in the last months of his life by the public reaction against socialism. Some people, he said, did not even know the difference between socialism and anarchy and yet automatically assumed both were wrong.[104] He was deeply disappointed that what had started so well during the war had ended so dismally after it. Before his death in May 1920, he was clearly disillusioned, and though his belief in the establishment of an American socialistic system may have been as strong as ever, his hopes for any immediate realization were completely shattered.

VIII

One more of Howells' social ideas deserves study. It is his proposal for a world government which would eventually end international strife. As early as May 1902, Howells, aroused by Cecil Rhodes' idea of a universal Anglo-Saxon empire, suggested "the federation of the world, in which every nation shall be equally a power" as "the only solidarity we can safely hope for." [105] These words may have been prompted by Howells' interest in the Hague Peace Conference of 1899 and the establishment of the Court of Arbitration in that same year. Both events represented a groping toward some kind of international cooperation, and Howells strongly approved of such activity.

But whether prompted by the meetings in The Hague or not, Howells' words show a very early attachment to international government. Though the concept of world union was an old one, talk of world federation was not common in 1902. For Howells to mention the idea reveals thought advanced beyond that of the early twentieth century.[106] However, he did not elaborate on his plan in other writings during the next few years. This one statement stands virtually alone until November 1914.[107] By this time, discussion of world union was widespread, and many societies that later were to give strong support to the League of Nations were already in existence.

In 1914, however, in an article aimed at nationalism, Howells brought forth a plan which, though theoretical and incomplete, embodied several notable features. He called for a "unification of mankind" and a "unity of the nations in some form of confederation."

We once thought it the finest possible thing that Italy should be unified, that Germany should be unified, that there should be a Pan-Slavic state, a Latin, a Teutonic entity. But it appears to us that history has been teaching, in her slow, patient way, that there is no unification worth having short of the unification of mankind whom God made of all one blood, and that until this is accomplished we have made no real advance in civilization or even Christianity.[108]

He wanted a single constitution

> which shall at first be so liberal as to admit all nations whether
> or not some of them still wish to deck themselves out with kings
> and nobles and such vain gauds, for a time, but shall finally in-
> tend only a republican form of government, as with the States
> of this our own happy Union.[109]

He believed that secession from the union should be frowned
upon but allowed and, finally, that a kind of cosmopolitan
brotherhood should supersede narrow nationalisms.

> When it comes to a question of our country as against any other
> country it seems to many of us that we proclaim a sentiment
> worthy of the deity in declaring for "our country right or wrong,"
> whereas it is a survival from the cave-dwelling cannibal of the
> stone age who lurks somewhere in the background of every
> human being. . . . what we ought really to think and feel and
> say is "Our country right; but when wrong, any country before
> her which is right". . . . national honor, a figment of mere ro-
> mance, which co-exists with national greed, national falsehood,
> national dishonesty, and all the other things that dishonor a man,
> is of the first importance in the imagination of unified national-
> ities. What we want now, therefore, is the unification of the
> species.[110]

"A unification of the species"—this is what Howells looked toward. Universal brotherhood was infinitely more important than
patriotism. "What we are contending for in all this," he wrote,
"is universality, the identity of men in their human character-
istics, and not in their racial, national, ancestral peculiarities." [111]

In this way Howells' idealism and humanism carry him to a
plan of world union, a plan by which the nations could eventually form a universal federation of republics. He mentions the
idea again in November 1916 when he urges a republican Europe.[112] Both articles and his use of the term "federation of the
world" seem to place him on the side of those who envisioned
the new alliance as patterned after the federal government of
the United States and having direct power over member states
rather than with those who saw the union as an organization of

sovereign states, a league whose power derived from treaty obligations and public opinion instead of sovereignty itself. Howells, however, never really probed the basic question of the structure of an international organization, and after 1916 he did not mention the topic again, even though the Covenant of the League of Nations was warmly debated in the United States in 1919 and 1920. Howells was ill much of this time, and most of his efforts were concentrated on completing the outline for the second volume of his autobiography, *Years of My Middle Life.*

It is clear, however, that Howells favored world union and made his support known during the twentieth century. He wished to express his views on this subject as he had on prison reform, arbitration, and monopoly; and it seems obvious that he saw himself as a social observer in the twentieth century as well as in the nineteenth. One had a duty, he thought, to work and strive for what he believed was right; this was the way progress came about. If one was to be a realist and write about his own time and environment, he could not avoid comment on contemporary society. These convictions always remained with Howells, and his remarks on reform, as scattered and unconsecutive as they sometimes are, form a signficant part of his writing. One cannot dismiss them without losing in the process an important phase of Howells' thought.

7

HOWELLS' ROLE IN REFORM THOUGHT

IN CONSIDERING Howells' place in the reform movement of his day, one should look first at his audience. How many people did Howells reach? Did this number change during his lifetime? What *kind* of an audience did he have? These are legitimate questions.

William Dean Howells was read by millions of Americans. With the exception of Mark Twain, he was undoubtedly the most widely read author in America between 1880 and 1895. To young Hamlin Garland, Howells was indisputably the chief figure in American literature, and his books and articles "were being read aloud in thousands of home circles." [1] Any precise estimate of the number of these home circles, however, is tentative at best. Harper's, the publishing house which printed every one of Howells' important social books and with whom Howells worked almost exclusively from 1887 to 1916, had several fires early in the twentieth century, and consequently there is no complete set of sales records on Howells' works until after 1915 and almost no figures at all on his books before 1900. [2]

Fortunately, one can gain a more reliable estimate on another part of Howells' audience—those who read his novels in serialized form before book publication. The magazines which carried Howells' stories included *Harper's Monthly,* which serialized *Annie Kilburn* in 1888 and *The World of Chance* in 1892 (circulation 160,000 in 1897);[3] *Harper's Weekly,* which ran *A Hazard of New Fortunes* in 1899 (circulation 80,000 in 1897);[4] *Cosmopolitan,* which printed *A Traveler from Altruria* in 1892 and the first part of *Through the Eye of the Needle* in 1893 (circulation 250,000 in 1897);[5] and *Century,* which serialized *The Minister's Charge* in 1886 (circulation 160,000 in 1897).[6] The New York *Sun,* a newspaper which serialized *The Quality of Mercy* in 1891, had approximately 110,000 readers in 1897.[7]

These figures indicate that, with the exception of *A Hazard of New Fortunes,* every one of Howells' important social novels was available to over 100,000 readers before book publication, and if one multiplies these circulation figures by four or five, the number of people who probably read each circulated copy, the figures reach impressive totals. These totals also are relevant for Howells' articles, which were usually printed in magazines before being collected into books. How many subscribers and their friends read Howells' articles and serials is another question, but most scholars believe that magazine readers in the nineteenth century usually read the entire issue—essays, stories, serials, jokes, and all—and were much less selective in their reading than modern audiences.[8] It seems obvious that Howells reached a large number of his contemporaries.

After the turn of the century, however, Howells' audience grew smaller. Though the number of his readers always remained respectable, his novels sold less well, and, after the publication of *The Son of Royal Langbrith* in 1904, they were no longer serialized in magazines. His articles also reached a more limited audience because of the noticeable decline in Harper's magazines in the first two decades of the twentieth century. Because of an exclusive contract with Harper's, Howells could no longer contribute to *Century, Cosmopolitan, Scribner's,* and other periodicals which previously had brought him into contact with a larger number of readers. He did contribute to *Harper's Weekly* and the *North American Review* during these years, but their audiences were smaller than those of the journals for which he had formerly written. Thus in estimating Howells' audience, one must take into account two different periods—an earlier and a later. An article like "Letters of an Altrurian Traveler" (*Cosmopolitan,* November 1893) might have reached 750,000 readers, whereas the "Editor's Easy Chair" of November 1914 which discussed world unification may have been read by 250,000.[9]

All in all, these figures, approximate as they are, indicate that Howells had a sizeable reading public. Moreover, Howells' magazine public was an elite one. The periodicals that Howells wrote for—*Harper's Monthly, Century, North American Review, Scribner's*—were the most highly regarded in the country and were definitely intended for an intellectual audience. For Howells to have access to this audience meant that he was reaching an important and influential group of Americans—a group not open to every reformer. This fact, along with the number of his readers, gives Howells a unique place among liberal writers. Few sold so well or had so important a readership.

I I

The most significant fact about Howells' social writings is that they reflected and, more importantly, promoted many liberal ideas of the age. These ideas were not those of the majority at the time that Howells wrote, but the number of Howells-supported causes that eventually succeeded or exerted a strong influence on public opinion is surprisingly large. As we have seen, the major point in his prison reform, the payment of prisoners, won general acceptance after 1915. Women's suffrage became a part of the federal constitution in 1920. New federal laws on monopolies, income taxes, and labor practices were passed in the years between 1900 and 1916. The national park system and the conservation program expanded. Arbitration was officially adopted by the United States government. Anti-imperialism gained approval from a large and important minority. World union was supported by millions.

Most important of all, the whole concept of government shifted during Howells' lifetime. One of the most significant facts in American history is the tremendous expansion of governmental duties and responsibilities that occurred between the

pre-Civil War administration of James Buchanan, when Howells began writing, and the post-World War administration of
Woodrow Wilson, when he ended. The philosophy of government in the United States changed from that of the Jeffersonian
minimized state to that of the state as an active, intervening force
in the affairs of men—a change that Howells had advocated,
implicitly or explicitly, throughout his social writings.

Naturally, one cannot credit Howells with a major role in the
success of all these movements. On some of them he wrote very
little and only indicated his approval. But on others he wrote at
some length, and in the success of two, anti-imperialism and the
acceptance of great governmental activity, he played a considerable part. Undoubtedly one of the reasons that public control
of vital industries was so quietly accepted during the first World
War was the groundwork that such men as Howells, Bellamy,
and Henry Lloyd had been laying for thirty years. Because of
their efforts, public management was no longer the tremendous
bugaboo it had once been, and though undoubtedly not supported by everyone, it was tolerated by even its bitterest enemies
during the emergency.[10]

Howells also gave invaluable aid to the reform movement by
sponsoring and promoting the books of liberal writers. He was
personally responsible for getting Henry Lloyd's two vitally significant works, "Story of a Great Monopoly" and *Wealth Against
Commonwealth*, before the public. These two works began the
muckraking exposés which were to be so important in political
and economic reform. The first Howells accepted for the *Atlantic*
after it had been refused by the *North American Review*, and
the second he personally took to Henry Harper after Harper's and
three other publishing houses had rejected the manuscript. Lloyd
was beginning to despair of finding a publisher when he sent
the book to Howells in hopes of getting help. Howells convinced
Harper that the book should be published, and *Wealth Against
Commonwealth*, an exposé of the business practices of the
Standard Oil Company, became Lloyd's most important work.

By means of his reviews and comments in *Harper's Monthly*,
Howells also became an advance agent for the writings of other
reformers. In June 1888, he wrote an enthusiastic review of
Bellamy's *Looking Backward* which undoubtedly spurred the

sale of the book, particularly in the East, after mixed reviews and a poor sale had greeted the book in January. Three years later he did the same thing for Garland's *Main-Travelled Roads,* a realistic though austere picture of life on the prairie farms of the Midwest. This book, Garland said, had almost no sale until "Howells came to my support," but with his aid and that of others it "gradually made its way in the East." [11] In April and May 1899, Howells devoted two successive columns in *Literature* magazine to the commendation of a new work, *The Theory of the Leisure Class,* by an author, Thorstein Veblen, previously unknown to him. These articles, which stood almost alone in their praise of the book in 1899, gave a great impetus to the popularity of Veblen's study of the upper class. Joseph Dorfman, Veblen's biographer, remarks that Howells' reviews undoubtedly "helped to make the book a sensation" and to popularize such terms as "conspicuous consumption" and "pecuniary emulation." [12]

Besides assisting these more well-known critics of the established order, Howells also helped such an assorted group of reformers, writers, and economists as Laurence Gronlund, Richard T. Ely, Robert Herrick, Brand Whitlock, H. H. Boyesen, Abraham Cahan, and W. A. Wyckoff, all of whom had criticisms to make of American society. Often Howells found some of his own ideas echoed in these authors and was happy to praise their work. He described Ely as a political scientist who "denies that self-interest should be the ruling principle of life, and . . . will not allow us a moment's rest in the spoil of the stranger and the poor." [13] He thought that Gronlund was a "man to be read with respect," and that his plan of evolutionary socialism "cannot be ignored by any one who wishes to acquaint himself with the hopes and motives of a very intelligent body of men." [14]

But Howells went even beyond this. He included in his articles the views of foreign writers whose remarks had pertinence for American readers. We have seen how he publicized Tolstoy's writings in this country. To a lesser degree he did much the same thing for some of the works of Palacio Valdés, Ruskin, Morris, Ibsen, Shaw, and Balzac. When Palacio Valdés made some favorable comments on women's rights in 1911, Howells brought them to the attention of American readers: "As our friend Valdés shows in the most delightful of his *Papers of Doc-*

tor Angelico, woman has a genius for politics." [15] He gave the same treatment to Ibsen's study of civic corruption in *The Enemy of the People,* Morris' remarks on the tawdriness of commercial civilization, and Palacio Valdés' comments on the rapacity and greed of wealthy industrialists in *Scum.*[16] By such reviewing, Howells both encouraged his audience to read the books and gave himself a chance to comment on ideas which he felt had relevance to the American scene. In this way he not only introduced many European writers to America but brought their ideas to bear on the American reform movement.

Howells' promotion of liberal ideas performed an important service for the reform cause. As a columnist for *Harper's Monthly,* Howells called attention to authors and ideas that his readers would have encountered in few other magazines in America. Neither in the *Atlantic Monthly, Century, Scribner's,* nor any similar magazine is there anything parallel to his continual interest in progressive thought. The more sensational magazines, interested in exposés, were concerned primarily with uncovering rather than rectifying, but Howells' thought turned in a different direction. His appeal was to a different audience, and in a real sense he became the publicist, the promotor, for reform thought among cultivated American readers. His promotion was a significant contribution to the success of many new ideas.

III

From the vantage point of the mid-twentieth century, it is hard to realize that William Dean Howells was once a powerful voice in American literature. Today the man that Henry James called a "master" [17] and that Mark Twain believed as a stylist to be "without his peer in the English-writing world" [18] is little honored. His contribution to realism and his value as an observer are noted, but as an author of living merit he is all but ignored.

This fall from favor cannot be attributed completely to the fact that times and customs have moved away from Howells' Victorian morality and his insistence on commonplace reality. Certainly there is much to criticize in Howells. He never fully understood the emotional and subrational forces in man, and at times he was overly optimistic about human nature. He refused to probe some aspects of life. His reasoning was sometimes done in a void and he was not exempt from the fault of being logical rather than reasonable—an error he held against Tolstoy.[19]

Moreover, to a man of the twentieth century, Howells reveals at times an amazing naïveté. He apparently regarded socialism as the perfect end-all and seemed to have seen few of the problems that might arise from such a system. He believed that nineteen-twentieths of all crime came from economic want, and suggested that personal experience was not necessary for an understanding of evil, but that a reading of history could guide one's conduct.[20] These ideas, sincerely held by Howells, reveal the distance between him and contemporary times.

Yet with all this, there is still much to commend Howells. He saw the novel, indeed all writing, as an instrument of cultural advancement rather than solely as a means of entertainment, and acting within this concept, he strove to deal with the social and economic problems of his age. He saw, as some writers did not, the slums, the strikes, the effects of minimized government, the closing of the frontier, the results of cutthroat competition. In recommending governmental control of basic industries to correct these conditions, he was merely speaking out in the voice of that early equalitarian America where "nobody was very rich and nobody was in want." [21] True, he had to give up the idea of a minimized state, one ideal of this early society, but he knew that such a state was an anachronism in the 1880's. If America was to be the land of freedom and opportunity for all, he realized that it must have a government strong enough to enforce its will in an industrial age.

Since Howells' time, reform has flowed mainly in the channels he helped create. Social security, public housing, public employment, government-sponsored mediation between management and labor, public power, minimum wages, economic planning boards—these are all concepts that Howells would have delighted in. To be sure, America is still a capitalistic country and gives no sign of becoming a socialist Altruria, but in the last thirty years the United States government has assumed responsibilities for maintaining some degree of economic security for each of its citizens. Such an assumption represents a revolutionary change in American thought, and it is one which Howells foresaw and spoke for. A complete *laissez faire* philosophy is dead, probably never to be revived, and the words of Franklin D. Roosevelt on the eve of World War II—"I would ask no one to defend a democracy which in turn would not defend everyone in the nation against want and privation" [22]—echo those of Howells forty years before.

It is important to remember that the changes Howells recommended were all to be accomplished through the democratic process. This is one fact absolutely essential to the understanding of Howells. He was a thorough democrat, and he made his collective theories dependent upon the democratic tradition. Force and violence were absolutely foreign to his philosophy. If social progress could come only through revolution, it was not worth having. Howells, however, was sure that advancement could come through the polls. His faith in the American public wavered at times, but it never collapsed. Democracy, he knew, was only as strong as its voters, but he had confidence in the final wisdom of the people. There was room for misgivings about the democratic system, he said in 1909, but none for denial.[23]

In his plans for social reform, Howells allowed for evolution and compromise. He saw clearly that such radical changes as public control of industry and the establishment of women's suffrage could not come about overnight, and, though the wait was often painful, he realized that people had to be shown the benefits of the innovations. His job, as he conceived it, was to reveal the defects of the old and the virtues of the new. Then, if people agreed with him, changes could be set into motion. But he realized that one had to be patient.

The impact of Howells' ideas on his own era, though difficult to appraise accurately, was probably far greater than most modern historians recognize. Both as a novelist and as an essayist, Howells was read by millions over a long span of years, and he enjoyed a literary reputation probably unmatched by any other reform writer of his time. These facts gave him an obvious importance in the reform movement, a fact well recognized by those of his contemporaries who sought his support on specific measures.[24] Though his readership declined in the twentieth century, Howells' basic premises never changed, and together with such liberals as Herbert Croly, Walter Weyl, and Thorstein

Veblen, he continued to transmit social and economic attitudes which not only had an importance before World War I but represented a significant and vital opposition to the resurgence of the *laissez faire* business interests which began after the war. President Harding's pledge of a "return to normalcy" and President Coolidge's tolerant treatment of business gave a temporary victory to the "New Conservatives" during the 1920's, but reform ideas continued to live under the surface. The economic crisis of the Depression brought many of these concepts back into favor, and the New Deal utilized some of them in its program. There is no doubt that the executives and publicizers of the new program—the Roosevelts, the Brandeises, the Tugwells, the Lippmanns—were in a direct line of descent from Howells and his generation and eventually reaped a harvest sown during the Populist and muckraker days. The foothold provided by earlier liberals proved invaluable to the writers of the '20's and '30's, and one has only to read some of the later works to see the alliance between the two groups. In 1925 Rexford Tugwell, Thomas Munro, and Roy Stryker concluded their study of American economics—a study which included chapters on the cooperative movement, government ownership, and socialism—with these words:

> In cooperation alone, which depends upon the voluntary linking up of the individual with the groups through which he necessarily functions, and upon his merging of his interests with those of his group, were we able to see a possible suggestion of future development. Cooperation might be called *voluntary socialism*, for that is what it is. We . . . asked for it the consideration of the generation to which this book is addressed.[25]

Finally, Howells brought a significant standard of values to bear on the economic and social questions of his day. With his belief in a democratic polity and the rational capacity of man, he sought to expose and correct some of the lesions in the American system which the industrial age had brought. Basically a son of the Enlightenment, he wanted to shape the social and natural environment with the intelligence that man had at his command. It is obvious that some of Howells' solutions would not meet approval today, but his approach to the problem, his belief in human intelligence and the ultimate ability of man to choose wisely if properly informed, is firmly in a humanistic tradition which still has validity.

> We can use our wit and our force to make footholds for reason. Behind our pictures of the world, we can try to see the vista of a longer duration of events, and . . . allow this longer time to control our decisions. . . . The more realistically men have faced out the brutality and the hysteria, the more they have earned the right to say that it is not foolish for men to believe . . . that intelligence, courage, and effort cannot ever contrive a good life for all men.[26]

These are the words of Walter Lippmann. They are the thoughts of William Dean Howells.

NOTES

CHAPTER 1

INTRODUCTION

[1] See William Dean Howells, *Literary Friends and Acquaintance* (New York: Harper & Bros., 1901), 55.

[2] See William Dean Howells, *Life in Letters*, ed. Mildred Howells (Garden City, N. Y.: Doubleday, Doran, & Co., 1928), II, 365.

[3] As quoted in Newton Arvin, "The Usableness of Howells," *New Republic*, XCI (June 30, 1937), 227.

[4] See Everett Carter, *Howells and the Age of Realism* (Philadelphia: J. B. Lippincott Co., 1954) and Gordon Haight, "Realism Defined: William Dean Howells," *Literary History of the United States*, ed. Robert Spiller and others (New York: Macmillan Co., 1948) II, 878-898.

[5] Arvin, *op. cit.*, 227-228.

[6] See particularly V. L. Parrington, Jr., *American Dreams* (Providence, R. I.: Brown University Press, 1947), 170-175.

[7] William Dean Howells, "Some Unpalatable Suggestions," *North American Review*, CLXXXVIII (May 1908), 258-259.

[8] See William Dean Howells, *My Literary Passions and Criticism and Fiction* (New York: Harper & Bros., 1910), 282.

CHAPTER 2

THE GOLDEN AGE

[1] William Cooper Howells, *Recollections of Life in Ohio from 1813 to 1840* (Cincinnati: Robert Clarke Co., 1895), 199. William Dean Howells wrote the introduction and final chapter of the book after his father died.

[2] The publishing house of Follett and Foster actually chose Howells for the job, but only after consulting with local Republicans.

[3] William Dean Howells, *A Boy's Town* (New York: Harper & Bros., 1890), 22.

[4] *Ibid.*, 14.

[5] See Edward Eggleston, *The Circuit Rider* (New York: Charles Scribner's Sons, 1903) for an accurate picture of this phase of the frontier and for typical sermons given by such preachers.

[6] William Dean Howells, *Years of My Youth* (New York: Harper & Bros., 1916), 83.

[7] William Cooper Howells, *op. cit.*, 145.

[8] Henry Steele Commager, *The American Mind* (New Haven: Yale University Press, 1950), 29.

[9] See William Dean Howells, *New Leaf Mills* (New York: Harper & Bros., 1913), 91, and *A Boy's Town*, 50, respectively.

[10] See Edward Eggleston, *The Hoosier Schoolmaster* (New York: Macmillan Co., 1928), 34-46, and *The Circuit Rider*, 10-29.

[11] William Dean Howells, *Literary Friends and Acquaintance*, 3.

[12] See Merle Curti, *The Growth of American Thought* (New York: Harper & Bros., 1943), 357.

[13] William Dean Howells, *Stories of Ohio* (New York: American Book Co., 1897), 212.

[14] See Howells, *Years of My Youth*, 18, 90.

[15] *Ibid.*, 205.

[16] Thomas H. Huxley, *Science and Culture and Other Essays* (New York: Appleton and Co., 1890), 22.

[17] Curti, *op. cit.*, 108.

[18] Howells, *Life in Letters*, I, 417.

[19] As quoted in Allan Nevins, *The Emergence of Modern America 1865 to 1878*, Vol. VIII of *A History of American Life*, ed. Arthur Schlesinger and Dixon Ryan Fox (12 vols.; New York: Macmillan Co., 1928), 32.

[20] See V. L. Parrington, *Main Currents in American Thought* (New York: Harcourt, Brace, & Co., 1930), III, 33, 34.

21 *Ibid.*, 39, 43.

22 Ralph Arnold and William Kemnitzer, *Petroleum in the United States and Possessions* (New York: Harper & Bros., 1931), 42. Similar though less spectacular growth was apparent in other industries. For a good view of the whole phenomenon of industrial expansion after the Civil War, see Allan Nevins, *op. cit.*

23 See Henry Adams, *The Education of Henry Adams* (New York: Houghton Mifflin Co., 1918), 53.

24 *Ibid.*, 237.

CHAPTER 3

HOWELLS AND THE *ATLANTIC*

1 See, for example, Howells' article on labor in the *Nation*, II (March 1866), 261.

2 See Howells' picture of Cambridge life in *Literary Friends and Acquaintance*, 179 ff.

3 See particularly the description of the Irish settlement in *Suburban Sketches* (New York: Hurd & Houghton, 1871), 64-74.

4 For a more extended investigation of Howells' editorship of the *Atlantic Monthly*, see L. J. Budd's "Howells, the *Atlantic Monthly*, and Republicanism," *American Literature*, XXIV (May 1952), 139-156. I am indebted to Professor Budd for much of the information contained in this section.

5 See *Atlantic Monthly*, XXVIII (July 1871), 1-128.

6 See respectively *Atlantic Monthly*, XXXIII (January 1874), 92-101; (April 1874), 441-452; (January 1874), 59-68; (June 1874), 697-712; (June 1874), 730-736.

7 As quoted in L. J. Budd, "Howells, the *Atlantic Monthly*, and Republicanism," *American Literature*, XXIV (May 1952), 146.

8 See *Atlantic Monthly*, XXX (July 1872), 127-128, and XXX (November 1872), 638-640.

9 See respectively R. T. Ely, "German Cooperative Credit Unions," *Atlantic Monthly*, XLVII (February 1881), 207-223; G. E. Waring, "Life and Work of the Eastern Farmer," *Atlantic Monthly*, XXXIX (May 1877), 584-595; and G. W. Julian, "Our Land Policy," *Atlantic Monthly*, XLIII (March 1879), 325-337.

10 See respectively *Atlantic Monthly*, XLIII (May 1879), 602-609; XLIII (April 1879), 497-500; XLV (January 1880), 19-32; XLIV (October 1879), 521-532; XLVI (December 1880), 787-792.

11 See Willard Brown, "Socialism in Germany," *Atlantic Monthly*, XLIV (October 1879), 532.

[12] See William Dean Howells, "A New Observer," *Atlantic Monthly*, XLV (June 1880), 848-849.

[13] During his editorship, Howells naturally made other statements concerning American society, but almost always they were general rather than specific. For example, in his review of Henry James' *Hawthorne* (*Atlantic Monthly*, XLV [February 1880], 282-285), Howells writes that the American social structure presents the only fresh opportunities left to fiction. He obviously approves of the general equalitarianism here, particularly when compared with the state of social classes in England, but he does not venture further into social commentary. This attitude is typical of Howells' own writing in the *Atlantic*. For other general remarks on society, see "Recent Literature," XXXIII (February 1874) 231-235; "Mr. Parkman's Histories," XXXIV (November 1874) 602-610; and "A French Poet of the Old Regime," XLI (March 1878), 332-343.

[14] This emphasis is typical of the magazine's position during these years. Both groups were to blame, but labor was the more culpable. See Edward Atkinson's "The Unlearned Profession," *Atlantic Monthly*, XLV (June 1880), 742-753.

[15] Howells, "A New Observer," 848.

[16] *Ibid.*

[17] *Ibid.*

[18] For previous criticism, see particularly Charles Seymour, "A Western View of Inter-State Transportation," *Atlantic Monthly*, XXX (September 1872), 345-351.

[19] See Caroline Lloyd, *Henry Demarest Lloyd* (New York: G. P. Putnam's Sons, 1912), 1, 59-62.

[20] Lloyd first offered the article to the *North American Review*, but the editor, Allen Thorndike Rice, refused it, probably because of its explosive nature.

[21] As quoted in L. J. Budd, "Howells, the *Atlantic Monthly*, and Republicanism," 150.

[22] See particularly William Dean Howells, *Dr. Breen's Practice* (Boston: Houghton Mifflin Co., 1881), 265-266.

[23] See respectively William Dean Howells, *A Modern Instance* (New York: Houghton Mifflin Co., 1922), 229, 297-299, 302-303.

[24] See Howells, *Years of My Youth*, 201.

[25] Howells, *Atlantic Monthly*, XLV, 849.

[26] William Dean Howells, "Police Report," *Atlantic Monthly*, XLIX (January 1882), 16.

[27] William Dean Howells, "Recent American Novels, 'The Breadwinners,'" *Century*, XXVIII (May 1884), 153.

[28] Marrion Wilcox, "The Works of William Dean Howells," *Harper's Weekly*, XL (July 4, 1896), 656.

[29] See Everett Carter, *Howells and the Age of Realism*, 170-224, and L. J. Budd, "Howells' Debt to Tolstoy," *American Slavic and Eastern European Review*, IX (1950), 292-301.

[30] See G., "Mr. Howells' Socialism," *American Fabian*, IV (February 1898), 2.

[31] Howells, *Life in Letters*, I, 372-3.

[32] See William Dean Howells, "Editor's Study," *Harper's Monthly*, LXXIV (February 1887), 482-486.

[33] See William Dean Howells, "Lyof Tolstoy," *Harper's Weekly*, XXXI (April 23, 1887), 299-300.

[34] See William Dean Howells, "Editor's Study," *Harper's Monthly*, LXXIV (May 1887), 983-987.

[35] See William Dean Howells, "Editor's Study," *Harper's Monthly*, LXXV (July 1887), 315-320.

[36] See William Dean Howells, "Editor's Study," *Harper's Monthly*, LXXV (August 1887), 476-480.

[37] See William Dean Howells, "Editor's Study," *Harper's Monthly*, LXXV (October 1887), 801-806.

[38] As quoted in Leonard Lutwack, "William Dean Howells and the 'Editor's Study,'" *American Literature*, XXIV (June 1952), 198.

[39] Budd, "Howells' Debt to Tolstoy," 295.

[40] Howells, *A Boy's Town*, 11.

[41] See respectively Howells, *New Leaf Mills*, 35, and *A Boy's Town*, 151 and 12.

[42] Howells, *My Literary Passions and Criticism and Fiction*, 183, 184.

[43] William Dean Howells, "In Honor of Tolstoy," *Critic*, XXX (October 1898), 288.

[44] Edward Everett Hale, Jr., *The Life and Letters of Edward Everett Hale* (Boston: Little, Brown, & Co., 1917), II, 327-328.

[45] See William Dean Howells, *The World of Chance* (New York: Harper & Bros., 1893), 90.

[46] This latter idea, of course, plays an important role in the story of Levin and Kitty in *Anna Karenina* and is one that Howells specifically mentions in his review of Tolstoy's *Que Faire?* in 1887. See his "Editor's Study," *Harper's Monthly*, LXXV (July 1887), 316.

[47] William Dean Howells, *The Minister's Charge* (Boston: Houghton Mifflin Co., 1887), 240-241.

[48] *Ibid.*, 184.

[49] *Ibid.*, 237.

[50] *Ibid.*, 458, 459.

[51] *Ibid.*, 182, 186.

[52] Howells, *Life in Letters*, I, 393.

[53] *Ibid.*, I, 397.

[54] See Brand Whitlock's account, quoted in *Life in Letters*, I, 400.

[55] Howells, *Life in Letters*, I, 399.

[56] *Ibid.*, I, 402.

[57] Edwin Cody, *The Realist at War* (Syracuse, N. Y.: Syracuse University Press, 1958), 74.

[58] Howells, *Life in Letters*, I, 404.

[59] *Ibid.*

[60] *Ibid.*, 407, 8.

[61] See Walter Fuller Taylor, "Howells' Interest in Economic Reform," *American Literature*, II (March 1930), 7.

[62] See Howells, *Life in Letters*, I, 411.

[63] *Ibid.*, I, 413-414.

[64] *Ibid.*, I, 416.

[65] *Ibid.*, I, 417.

[66] *Ibid.*, I, 418.

[67] William Dean Howells, *Annie Kilburn* (New York: Harper & Bros., 1889), 24.

[68] *Ibid.*, 240.

CHAPTER 4

HOWELLS AND REFORM: 1888–1896

[1] Henry Steele Commager, *The American Mind*, viii.

[2] See John Hicks, *A Short History of American Democracy* (Boston: Houghton Mifflin Co., 1946), 538.

[3] See particularly his comments on individualism, Christian Society, and civic duties in *Harper's Monthly*, LXXIX (August 1889), 476-481; LXXX (February 1890), 480-485; and LXXXII (January 1891), 316-321, respectively.

[4] The first half of *Through the Eye of the Needle* was originally published as "Letters of an Altrurian Traveler" in *Cosmopolitan* magazine for November 1893.

[5] William Dean Howells, *Through the Eye of the Needle* (New York: Harper & Bros., 1907), 219. See also the Altrurian's comments in *A Traveler from Altruria* (New York: Harper & Bros., 1894), 29, 296, 310, and 316.

[6] William Graham Sumner, "The Absurd Attempt to Make the

World Over," *War and Other Essays* (New Haven: Yale University Press, 1911), 198, 209.

[7] Lester Ward, *Dynamic Sociology* (New York: Appleton & Co., 1883), II, 632-633.

[8] Howells, *Impressions and Experiences* (New York: Harper & Bros., 1909), 32.

[9] *Ibid.*, 106.

[10] *Ibid.*, 110.

[11] William Dean Howells, *A Hazard of New Fortunes* (New York: Harper & Bros., 1890), I, 297.

[12] William Dean Howells, *The Quality of Mercy* (New York: Harper & Bros., 1892), 262-263.

[13] *Ibid.*, 14.

[14] *Ibid.*, 14-15.

[15] *The Minister's Charge*, 457 ff.

[16] Howells, *The Quality of Mercy*, 161.

[17] *Ibid.*, 474.

[18] Howells, *My Literary Passions and Criticism and Fiction*, 138-139.

[19] William Dean Howells, *An Imperative Duty* (New York: Harper & Bros., 1892), 38-39.

[20] Howells, *A Traveler from Altruria*, 61.

[21] See *A Traveler from Altruria*, 283 ff., and *Through the Eye of the Needle*, 131 ff.

[22] For specific comment see Howells, *Annie Kilburn*, 65, 231-233, *The Minister's Charge*, 37, and *A Hazard of New Fortunes*, I, 307, 8.

[23] See *Annie Kilburn*, 262.

[24] Howells, *Annie Kilburn*, 240.

[25] Howells, *An Imperative Duty*, 26.

[26] *Ibid.*, 27.

[27] *Ibid.*

[28] William Dean Howells, "Equality as the Basis of Good Society," *Century*, XXIX (November 1895), 65-66.

[29] *Ibid.*, 67.

[30] Howells, *A Hazard of New Fortunes*, II, 251, 253.

[31] William Dean Howells, "Who Are Our Brethren?" *Century*, LI (April 1896), 935-936.

[32] See *A Traveler from Altruria*, 262.

[33] See for example Alexander Harvey, *William Dean Howells* (New York: B. W. Huebsch, 1917), 166-168.

[34] C. Hartley Grattan, *American Mercury*, XX, 45.

CHAPTER 5
SOCIAL COMMENTARY

[1] Howells, *Forum*, XX, 407.

[2] *Ibid.*, 404.

[3] *Ibid.*, 408.

[4] *Ibid.*, 409.

[5] Howells, *Century*, XXIX, 67.

[6] *Ibid.*

[7] Howells, *Century*, LI, 933.

[8] Howells, *Annie Kilburn*, 12.

[9] Howells, *Century*, LI, 933.

[10] See particularly Howells' use of the term on pages 405-409.

[11] Howells, *Annie Kilburn*, 241.

[12] Howells, *A Traveler from Altruria*, 271.

[13] Howells, *The World of Chance*, 119.

[14] Howells, *Century*, XXIX, 66.

[15] *Ibid.*, 67.

[16] See *Century*, XXIX, 65-67. Note also Howells' praise of men who have risen from humble beginnings, "Editor's Easy Chair," *Harper's Monthly*, CIV (January 1902), 334-338.

[17] Howells, *North American Review*, CLVIII, 191.

[18] *Ibid.*, 196.

[19] Howells, *A Traveler from Altruria*, 316.

[20] *Ibid.* See also 295-296.

[21] Howells, *Century*, LI, 935.

[22] Howells, *Through the Eye of the Needle*, 171.

[23] Howells, *A Traveler from Altruria*, 299.

[24] *Ibid.*, 300.

[25] *Ibid.*, 282.

[26] Howells, *Life in Letters*, II, 242.

[27] See particularly V. L. Parrington, Jr., *American Dreams*, 170-175.

[28] Howells, "Life and Letters," *Harper's Weekly*, XXXIX (August 31, 1895), 820.

[29] Howells, *Life in Letters*, II, 25.

[30] *Ibid.*, II, 26.

[31] Howells, *A Traveler from Altruria*, 223-224, 225.

[32] Howells, "Life and Letters," *Harper's Weekly*, XXIX (August 31, 1895), 820.

[33] Howells, *North American Review*, CLVIII, 194.

[34] *Ibid.*

[35] See *A Traveler from Altruria*, 271.

[36] See *The World of Chance*, 120.

[37] For an excellent discussion of the safety valve theory, see Henry Nash Smith, *Virgin Land* (Cambridge: Harvard University Press, 1950), 201-210.

[38] See the irate words of Reuben Camp, an Eastern farmer, in *A Traveler from Altruria*, 140.

[39] See Nevins, *The Emergence of Modern America 1865-1878*, 119.

[40] See Howells, *North American Review*, CLVIII, 194.

[41] *Ibid.*

[42] See Howells, *Life in Letters*, II, 3.

[43] Howells, *A Traveler from Altruria*, 141. See also Howells' remarks in "Our Special Wonder," *Harper's Weekly*, XLVI (June 24, 1902), 811.

[44] William Dean Howells, "A Boston Letter," *Critic*, XIX (January 14, 1893), 22.

[45] See Howells, *A Traveler from Altruria*, 196, 276.

[46] *Ibid.*, 198.

[47] Howells, *A Hazard of New Fortunes*, II, 252.

[48] Howells, *A Traveler from Altruria*, 276.

[49] Howells, *A Hazard of New Fortunes*, II, 213, 4.

[50] *Ibid.*, 214-215.

[51] See Howells, "Without Our Special Wonder," *Harper's Weekly*, XLVI (June 24, 1902), 811.

[52] See Howells, "Life and Letters," *Harper's Weekly*, XXXIX (September 7, 1895), 844.

[53] See Howells, *Impressions and Experiences*, 94-110.

[54] *Ibid.*, 110.

[55] See Eric Goldman, *Rendezvous with Destiny* (New York: Alfred Knopf, 1953), ix.

[56] Howells, *A Traveler from Altruria*, 264-271.

[57] Howells, *The World of Chance*, 125.

[58] Howells, *Century*, LI, 935.

[59] Howells, *The World of Chance*, 91.

[60] *Ibid.*, 125.

[61] *Ibid.*, 123, 124.

[62] See Howells, *Through the Eye of the Needle*, 231.

[63] Howells, *The World of Chance*, 246.

[64] Howells, *Life in Letters*, I, 418.

[65] See Howells, *Stories of Ohio*, 203-205.

[66] *Ibid.*

[67] See Howells' letter to Sylvester Baxter in *Life in Letters*, II, 69.

[68] *Ibid.*

CHAPTER 6

HOWELLS AND REFORM: 1896–1920

[1] See Van Wyck Brooks, *New England: Indian Summer* (New York: E. P. Dutton & Co., 1940), 390.

[2] See William Eckstrom, "The Equalitarian Principle in the Fiction of William Dean Howells," *American Literature*, XXIV (March 1952), 40.

[3] See, for examples, Howells' comments in "An Anxious Inquiry," *Harper's Weekly*, XLVI (May 24, 1902), 651, and the "Editor's Easy Chair," *Harper's Monthly*, CXXV, 634-637.

[4] Howells, *Atlantic Monthly*, XLV, 849.

[5] William Dean Howells, "American Letter," *Literature*, III (November 19, 1898), 475.

[6] *Ibid.*

[7] Howells, *Life in Letters*, II, 90.

[8] *Ibid.*, II, 89, 90.

[9] See particularly his letters in *Life in Letters*, II, 91 and 93. In both Howells discusses the war without any hint of imperialism.

[10] As quoted in Harold Faulkner, *The Quest for Social Justice 1898-1914*, Vol. XI of *A History of American Life*, ed. Arthur Schlesinger and Dixon Ryan Fox (12 vols.; New York: Macmillan Co., 1931), 312.

[11] Howells, *Life in Letters*, II, 95.

[12] Howells, "Our Spanish Prisoners," in *Literature and Life*, 143. The original title of the article was "Our Spanish Prisoners at Portsmouth," but when Howells incorporated it into his book, he shortened the title.

[13] *Ibid.*

[14] William Dean Howells, "Editor's Easy Chair," *Harper's Monthly*, CII (April 1901), 805. All references to the "Editor's Easy Chair" will be those written by Howells.

[15] "Editor's Easy Chair," *Harper's Monthly*, CII (May 1901), 967.

[16] William Dean Howells, "An Earlier American," *North American Review*, CLXXII (June 1901), 940, 942-943.

[17] "Editor's Easy Chair," *Harper's Monthly*, CIV (January 1902), 338.

[18] William Dean Howells, "The Turning of the Dove," *Harper's Weekly*, XLVI (February 8, 1902), 165.

[19] Howells, *My Literary Passions and Criticism and Fiction*, 282.

[20] William Dean Howells, "Race-Patriotism," *Harper's Weekly*, XLVI (May 10, 1902), 585.

[21] William Dean Howells, "Some Modest Misgivings," *Harper's Weekly*, XLVI (July 19, 1902), 946.

[22] William Dean Howells, "The Christmas Spirit," *Harper's Weekly*, XLVI (December 6, 1902), 1824.

[23] See "Editor's Easy Chair," *Harper's Monthly*, CVIII (March 1904), 640-644, and "Editor's Easy Chair," *Harper's Monthly*, CX (April 1905), 803-806.

[24] William Dean Howells, *Familiar Spanish Travels* (New York: Harper & Bros., 1913), 304.

[25] See Howells, *Life in Letters*, II, 361.

[26] As quoted in Curti, *The Growth of American Thought*, 571.

[27] As quoted in Henry Steele Commager, *The American Mind*, 209.

[28] William Dean Howells, "A Suggestion from the Boer War," *Harper's Weekly*, XLVI (June 10, 1902), 747.

[29] See "Editor's Easy Chair," *Harper's Monthly*, CVIII (March 1904), 641.

[30] *Ibid.*

[31] "Editor's Easy Chair," *Harper's Monthly*, CXV (March 1904), 641.

[32] William Dean Howells, "Life and Letters," *Harper's Weekly*, XL (January 4, 1896), 7.

[33] Howells, *Harper's Monthly*, CXV, 966.

[34] *Ibid.*, 968.

[35] "Editor's Easy Chair," *Harper's Monthly*, CXXIII (August 1911), 473.

[36] *Ibid.*

[37] William Dean Howells, "John Brown after Fifty Years," *North American Review*, CXCIII (January 1911), 33.

[38] See Howells' words on the Germans, "Editor's Easy Chair," *Harper's Monthly*, CXXXVII (August 1918), 444-446.

[39] Gibson and Arms, *Americana*, XXXVII (March 1943), 288.

[40] See William Dean Howells, "Life and Letters," *Harper's Weekly*, XL (February 22, 1896), 175.

[41] William Dean Howells, "Life and Letters," *Harper's Weekly*, XL (February 29, 1896), 199.

[42] *Ibid.*

[43] *Ibid.*

[44] See Norman Hapgood's account of the theatrical trust in his *The Stage in America 1879-1900* (New York: Macmillan, 1901), 6-38.

[45] As quoted in Hapgood, *The Stage in America*, 17.

[46] William Dean Howells, "Life and Letters," *Harper's Weekly*, XLII (February 26, 1898), 202.

[47] *Ibid.*

[48] Howells, *Harper's Weekly*, XL, 199.

[49] For his comments on equality, see *The Landlord at Lion's Head* (New York: Harper & Bros., 1897), 29 and 377. For those on the middle class, see pages 70 and 149.

[50] William Dean Howells, "Our Spanish Prisoners," in *Literature and Life* (New York: Harper & Bros., 1901), 314.

[51] See Howells, *Years of My Youth*, 41.

[52] William Dean Howells, *Seven English Cities* (New York: Harper & Bros., 1909), 5.

[53] See Howells, *Literary Friends and Acquaintance*, 58.

[54] See respectively Howells, *My Literary Passions and Criticism and Fiction*, 104, and *Literature and Life*, 1.

[55] See Howells, *Through the Eye of the Needle*, 228.

[56] See respectively Howells, *Through the Eye of the Needle*, 220, and *Imaginary Interviews* (New York: Harper & Bros., 1910), 5.

[57] See William Dean Howells, "Execution by Electricity," *Harper's Weekly*, XXXII (January 14, 1888), 23.

[58] See Howells, *The Quality of Mercy*, particularly the discussion between Matt and his father, 166 ff.

[59] See William Dean Howells, "Minor Topics," *Nation*, II (April 26, 1866), 517.

[60] As reprinted in "Personals," *Literary Digest*, XX (April 7, 1900), 438.

[61] William Dean Howells, "State Manslaughter," *Harper's Weekly*, XLVIII (February 6, 1904), 198.

[62] *Ibid.*

[63] William Dean Howells, "Diversions of the Higher Journalist, an Eye for an Eye," *Harper's Weekly*, XLVII (October 24, 1903), 1696.

[64] "Editor's Easy Chair," *Harper's Monthly*, CXXX (March 1915), 635.

[65] *Ibid.*, 636.

[66] William Dean Howells, "Some Unpalatable Suggestions," *North American Review*, CLXXVIII (August 1908), 256.

[67] See Howells, *Imaginary Interviews*, 171.

[68] Howells, *North American Review*, CLXXVIII, 258.

[69] *Ibid.*, 256-257.

[70] See W. T. Cross, "Jails and the Misdemeanant," *Survey*, XXXV (October 23, 1915), 93-94.

[71] "Editor's Easy Chair," *Harper's Monthly*, CXXIX (September 1914), 634-637.

[72] See Howells, *North American Review*, CLXXVIII, 256-257.

[73] *Ibid.*, 260.

[74] See Howells, *Harper's Monthly*, CXXIX, 634-637.

[75] *Ibid.*

[76] See H. E. Barnes and N. K. Teeter, *New Horizons in Criminology* (2d ed., New York: Prentice-Hall, 1951), chapters 25-28.

[77] Faulkner, *The Quest for Social Justice 1898-1914*, 173.

[78] William Dean Howells, *London Films* (New York: Harper & Bros., 1906), 72-73.

[79] "Editor's Easy Chair," *Harper's Monthly*, CXI (October 1905), 796.

[80] "Editor's Easy Chair," *Harper's Monthly*, CXVIII (May 1909), 967.

[81] Howells, *Literature and Life*, 21.

[82] "Editor's Easy Chair," *Harper's Monthly*, CXXVIII (June 1913), 151. As Howells grew older, he became inconsistent in his views on the democratic masses. Here he refers to them as "the ignorant and vicious majority," and he seems to share the disillusion of others in the early twentieth century concerning the people's capacity for right action. At other times he displays his old optimism, though he is never so confident as he was in the 1860's and '70's. For an example of his later optimism, see the "Editor's Easy Chair," *Harper's Monthly*, CXXXVI (February 1918), 450-453.

[83] "Editor's Easy Chair," *Harper's Monthly*, CXXIV (February 1912), 474. For more comment on women's spiritual superiority, see "Editor's Easy Chair," *Harper's Monthly*, CXI (October 1905), 794-797.

[84] See "Editor's Easy Chair," *Harper's Monthly*, CXL (March 1920), 568.

[85] See William Dean Howells, "The Worst of Being Poor," *Harper's Weekly*, XLVI (March 1902), 261.

[86] "Editor's Easy Chair," *Harper's Monthly*, CXXXIV (January 1917), 291.

[87] See "Editor's Easy Chair," *Harper's Monthly*, CXXXVIII (April 1919), 714.

[88] See Howells, *Life in Letters*, II, 220.

[89] Note his attention to it in *Through the Eye of the Needle*, 231.

[90] William Dean Howells, "An Opportunity for American Fiction," *Literature*, n. s. 1 (May 1899), 385.

[91] See William Dean Howells, "The New Phase of the Labor Problem," *Harper's Weekly*, XLVI (April 26, 1902), 521. Note also Howells' recommendation of the vote in *Through the Eye of the Needle*, 220.

[92] Howells, *Harper's Weekly*, XLVI, 521.

[93] Howells, *London Films*, 69.

[94] *Ibid.*

[95] Howells, *Seven English Cities*, 199.

[96] See Howells, *Imaginary Interviews*, 357.

[97] See George Arms, "Howells' Unpublished Prefaces," *New England Quarterly*, XVII (December 1944), 589-591.

[98] "Editor's Easy Chair," *Harper's Monthly*, CXXXVI (April 1918), 756.

[99] "Editor's Easy Chair," *Harper's Monthly*, CXXXV (September 1917), 58.

[100] "Editor's Easy Chair," *Harper's Monthly*, CXXXVII (November 1918), 880.

[101] "Editor's Easy Chair," *Harper's Monthly*, CXL (April 1920), 712.

[102] *Ibid.*

[103] *Ibid.*

[104] See William Dean Howells, *Harper's Monthly*, CXXXVII, 880.

[105] Howells, *Harper's Weekly*, XLVI, 585.

[106] For the growth of the concept of the League of Nations see Theodore Marburg, *The Development of the League of Nations Idea* (New York: Macmillan Co., 1932), II, 763-788.

[107] Two articles, one in *Harper's Weekly* on February 27, 1904, and one in *Harper's Monthly*, November 1907, praise The Hague Tribunal for its work in settling international disagreement but make no comment on world government.

[108] "Editor's Easy Chair," *Harper's Monthly*, CXXIX (November 1914), 960-961.

[109] *Ibid.*, 961.

[110] *Ibid.*, 959, 961.

[111] *Ibid.*, 960.

[112] "Editor's Easy Chair," *Harper's Monthly*, CXXXIII (November 1916), 940.

CHAPTER 7

HOWELLS' ROLE IN REFORM THOUGHT

[1] Garland, *Roadside Meetings*, 55.

[2] The following figures on Howells' social fiction have been taken from a letter from Harper & Brothers, dated June 27, 1956. Any significant totals on *Annie Kilburn*, *The World of Chance*, and *Impressions and Experiences* have been lost.

A Hazard of New Fortunes (first published 1890): 2,240 copies sold from 1915 to 1929, when the book went out of print.

The Quality of Mercy (first published 1892): 6,600 copies sold from 1915 to 1921, when the book went out of print.

A Traveler from Altruria (first published 1894): 3,750 copies sold from 1915 to 1930, when the book went out of print.

Through the Eye of the Needle (first published 1907): 8,300 copies sold from 1915 to 1924, when the book went out of print.

To make any sort of estimate on a book's popularity immediately after its publication from these figures would be a risky venture, but the totals do show that Howells' stories were still being read long after they had been written. The figure for *The Quality of Mercy*, one of Howells' lesser known works, is especially surprising.

[3] *American Newspaper Annual* (Philadelphia: N. W. Ayres & Son, 1897), 567. This and the following figures are estimated circulations.

[4] *Ibid.*

[5] *Ibid.*, 550.

[6] *Ibid.*, 561.

[7] *Ibid.*, 564.

[8] In a personal conversation, Richard Altick, a man who has worked in nineteenth-century bibliography, pointed out that usually whole families read the magazines from cover to cover.

[9] Both figures are based on an estimate three times the circulation total, an estimate which most critics believe conservative.

[10] See Howells' comments in "Editor's Easy Chair," *Harper's Monthly*, CXXXVI (April 1918), 756.

[11] Garland, *Roadside Meetings*, 179.

[12] Joseph Dorfman, *Thorstein Veblen and His America* (New York: Viking Press, 1934), 179.

[13] William Dean Howells, "Editor's Study," *Harper's Monthly*, LXXX (February 1890), 484.

[14] William Dean Howells, "Editor's Study," *Harper's Monthly*, LXXVI (April 1888), 803.

[15] William Dean Howells, "Editor's Easy Chair," *Harper's Monthly*, CXXIV (February 1912), 472.

[16] See respectively "The Ibsen Influence," *Harper's Weekly*, XXXIX (April 27, 1895), 390; "Editor's Study," *Harper's Monthly*, LXXX (January 1890), 323; and "Editor's Study," *Harper's Monthly*, LXXXII (April 1891), 805-806.

[17] Henry James, "A Letter to William Dean Howells," *North American Review*, CXCV (April 1912), 561.

[18] Mark Twain, "William Dean Howells," *Harper's Monthly*, CXIII (July 1906), 221.

[19] See William Dean Howells, "Lyof Tolstoy," *North American Review*, CLXXXVIII (December 1908), 843.

[20] See Howells, *Imaginary Interviews*, 164.

[21] Howells, *A Boy's Town*, 22.

[22] Franklin Delano Roosevelt, "Fireside Chat," December 29, 1940 as quoted in Curti, *The Growth of American Thought*, 717.

[23] See Howells, *Seven English Cities*, 200.

[24] For efforts by Judge Pryor, Burr Todd, and Hamlin Garland to gain Howells' support for the Chicago anarchists, an authors' union, and the People's Party respectively, see *Life in Letters*, I, 294; II, 23; and Garland's *Roadside Meetings* (New York: Macmillan Co., 1930), 63-64.

[25] Rexford Tugwell, Thomas Munro, and Roy Stryker, *American Economic Life and the Means of Its Improvement* (New York: Harcourt, Brace, & Co., 1925), 594.

[26] Walter Lippmann, *Public Opinion* (New York: Harcourt, Brace & Co., 1922), 417-418. For a similar statement by Howells, see *The World of Chance*, 125.

INDEX